# CHOSEN FOR GOOD

# Chosen for Good

Peter Lewis, Roy Clements
and Greg Haslam

*Edited by*
Robert Horn

KINGSWAY PUBLICATIONS
EASTBOURNE

First published 1986



ISBN 0 86065 448 6



*Front cover design by Vic Mitchell*

Printed in Great Britain for
KINGSWAY PUBLICATIONS LTD
Lottbridge Drove, Eastbourne, E. Sussex BN23 6NT by
Richard Clay (The Chaucer Press) Ltd, Bungay, Suffolk
Typeset by CST, Eastbourne, E. Sussex.

## *Contents*


On and up from the Base Camp – Robert Horn 7
Walking Tall, Fallen Short – Peter Lewis 17
Loved with Everlasting Love – Peter Lewis 40
A Death to Abolish Death – Roy Clements 71
An Offer You Can't Refuse – Roy Clements 101
You'll Get There in the End – Greg Haslam 131
For Further Reading 158

# *Note*

The contents of this book arose from a 'Bible School' held by Barcombe Baptist Chapel, East Sussex. A six-cassette album is available, comprising the five original addresses plus one cassette of questions and answers. Details from BBC Cassettes, Crink House, Barcombe Mills, Nr. Lewes, East Sussex BN8 5BJ.

# *On and up from the Base Camp*

*by*

Robert Horn

Every Christian has problems. Some may give the impression that their lives are one long triumphal procession, but we suspect deep down that it is not as easy as that. After all, the great characters of Bible history all had their problems – from Adam onwards. It was not just the ordinary people who went astray, though the Bible does issue warnings to us from the sad examples of everyday people – such as the Israelites who experienced the exodus deliverance and then sinned in their desert journey (1 Cor 10:6, 11). The problems and failures of the great heroes of the faith are also recorded: think of Abraham and Moses, Samson and David.

It was the same in New Testament days. The ordinary church members had a problem in believing an ordinary servant girl, Rhoda, when she told them that God had answered their prayers and released Peter from prison (Acts 12:15). Or think of three typical problems that James mentions in his letter: the preferential treatment of the rich, the unbridled use of the tongue and the quarrels caused by coveting (Jas 2:1–4; 3:1–2; 4:1–3).

Even the apostles had problems. Remember how Peter failed to act 'in line with the truth of the gospel' in Antioch and had to be rebuked (Gal 2:14). Or listen in on the 'sharp disagreement' between Paul and Barnabas over what to do about John Mark who had deserted them (Acts 15:39).

Yes, Bible characters had their wanderings and wonderings. What then are our problems? How should we approach them? It would be easy to make a list of the problems that beset believers today. Here are a few examples for a start: problems of relationships, problems at home and at work, problems of assurance, of guidance, of prosperity or failure, of self-esteem and personal identity, problems about goals, problems of depression and loneliness, of trusting God in an age of doubt, of weakness . . . the list goes on and on.

The Christian world seems to be in business today to tackle such problems. Hence the seemingly endless stream of books, magazines, cassettes, videos, seminars, conferences, conventions and celebrations that claim to speak relevantly to these matters. 'How to' books proliferate from the Christian problem-solving industry. Every publisher must have his own book on marriage problems, single problems, depression problems, diet problems.

This is not all to be dismissed. Much is very helpful. We can probably all think of books or sermons that have come to our rescue on particular issues. And, of course, even a quick reading of the New Testament makes vividly clear that it too was in business to deal with troubles and perplexities. Jesus dealt with people's problems, as the Samaritan woman and the rich young man discovered (Jn 4:1-42; Mk 10:17-23). Most of the New Testament's letters devote half their space to practical questions in their readers' lives and churches. The Bible emphatically faces up to such down-to-earth situations.

When we read the New Testament, however, we are left with the sneaking feeling that its approach is somehow different from ours. It is not problem-orientated, though in a profound sense it is problem-solving. It is not difficulty-dominated, though it enables the disciple to overcome. It is not a 'how to' manual offering techniques, though it does give a way forward. It does not revolve around our felt needs like some counselling sessions, though it knows how to handle our needs.

What is the difference between the New Testament's approach and ours? Let me try to answer by two illustrations. We are often like inexperienced climbers about to set out on an expedition. Full of raw enthusiasm, we don't want to take time tediously surveying the whole mountain range. It is too laborious to set up all the possible supplies and emergency equipment which we might or might not need. We feel that we've got what it takes and, anyway, want to be on our way. We have read one or two autobiographies of others who have gone on ahead and they made it sound easy. So we set out one bright morning. We soon manage to conquer a few of the foothills and really feel we're making progress.

Then problems start. The mist closes in, our food runs low, we have no compass and no charts. Without a base camp, the expedition will come to grief. We were too short-term in our approach, and the long-term prospects suffer.

To take a second illustration, we are like students approaching an exam. We're pressed for time and not on top of the syllabus, still less the whole subject. We become nervous and know that we need help now. So we look for quick solutions. We seek answers to fill in those gaps of which, in our ignorance, we are vaguely aware. We want someone to solve our immediate maths problem. We look up a few quotations to pad out our English literature essay. By these means we may pass, but this tactic will give us no understanding or grasp of the principles of the subject. It will never make us at home in it, because it simply deals with a few random parts. It may answer a question or two today, but will give no basis from which to answer further questions next week or next year. It will certainly not give us the power to put knowledge into practice.

The New Testament puts things the other way round. It begins by surveying the ground and building the base camp. It stocks it with every item – food and equipment, maps and instructions, means of communication, emergency services and medical supplies – which we will need for the ascent. To take the other illustration, the New Testament starts by taking us through a lively and vital syllabus; it will not all seem relevant right now, but later on it will enable us to face and answer the questions which the examination of life will pose in each successive test.

How does it do this? Basically by introducing us to the ultimate realities. It cuts through our errors, half-truths and misunderstandings and brings us face to face with God and how he sees things. It defines, for example, the truth about ourselves. It unmasks what we are actually like, why we are as we are, what we can and cannot do, and what we are responsible for. It gives us the only reliable understanding of ourselves, because it sets us before our Maker.

It presents to us the truth about God, the great overlord of our destiny. It displays his power and majesty. It describes his plans and decrees. It demonstrates that his purposes determine the world's course and our individual story, that his are the promises that count and that he has the decisive say in all that goes on. It declares, moreover, that this God is for us and that he has chosen us for good – not for any good in us, but chosen for keeps to receive good from him.

It moves on to the truth about Jesus Christ, telling us the facts about his coming and telling us also their meaning. Most centrally, it shows him dying to turn away the just and justifiable wrath of God by accepting the penalty of our guilt. The Bible portrays him actually securing the rescue of sinners of every kind – people of every class and colour, from all over the world, from every one of the hastening centuries. It assures to all who trust in Christ the experience of new life and total pardon from God.

Then it comes to the truth about how God works in us, how he turns rebels into friends, aliens into children, lovers of self into lovers of God. The New Testament radiates the warming fact that, from the burnt-out ashes of our lives, God can reconstruct a temple in which he is happy to live. It tells how he does this by his gentle, welcome and irresistible entry into our lives.

Finally, lest we still harbour fears about the future, it offers us a preview of the end. It takes note of our doubts about whether we will make it to the end of the journey. It recognizes that we will wonder about what will happen if we fall and disappoint Christ. And it announces that the saints will go marching in, bloodied in the battle but unbowed, to their eternal home.

It is in the base camp of such stunning facts and truths that the Bible begins to handle our problems. Everything, as Paul told the Christians in Rome, revolves round God. Everything good about our life is *from God*. He is the origin, the Lord and giver of our existence, the governor of our every breath. He made us, he meets us, he reconciles us, he renews us, he rules us. There is nothing good about us that we have not received from him (1 Cor 4:7). We are the total debtors, he the sole donor.

Moreover, everything about our salvation is *through him*. It is by means of his Son's life and death that we are pardoned and adopted. It is by the resurrecting power of his Spirit that we have life. It is by means of his word that we know the truth and are set free. It is by his sustaining strength that we keep going. It is by his supernatural dynamic that the gospel advances. It is all through him.

Everything is also *to him* and for him. He designed us to live to the praise of his glory. He made us to please him and is busy remaking us to display, both now and in the coming ages, the incomparable wealth of his grace (Eph 1:6; 2:7). We are here for him, to serve his purposes, do his will and honour his Son each day.

God, from beginning to end – that is the perspective the Bible gives us: 'For from him and through him and to him are all things. To him be the glory for ever! Amen' (Rom 11:36). So how does that relate to our problems? You may have problems about yourself. Maybe you've never felt that you understood who and what you are. You remain a mystery to yourself. Why do you do the things you do? Why the gulf between what you are and what you want to be? And does your life have any significance anyway? Are you just a faceless statistic in the human crowd, just a back-row member of the congregation? Do you matter to anyone? Do you matter to God?

You may be anxious about assurance, low in self-esteem, aware that you are nobody special and not noticeably gifted. You are conscious of failures and weaknesses, feeling guilty about some past sins, doing your best, but unsure whether you qualify to break the bread and drink the wine at the Lord's table. You believe that God is love – but is he love to you? You know that Christ died and believe that he has done his part, but fret about whether you have done yours. This lack of assurance in turn creates a problem in your witness. If you were more convinced about God for yourself, you would be more courageous about the gospel for others. But you tremble to bear testimony to Jesus and that only compounds your sense of uselessness. You end by disparaging yourself, as you look at others who always seem to have winning ways in witness.

Or your problem may concern prayer. When God knows it all anyway, you won't be telling him anything new – so do you have to pray? Is prayer worth while? Surely prayer can't change God's mind; and, if it can't, why bother? And even if you do bother (as a Christian will), what if the person for whom you are praying is not destined to be saved anyway?

The question of guidance may be bothering you. It may be a 'how to' question: how to find God's will, how to read circumstances, how to choose between this job or that. It may be the deeper question, you being the kind of person you are, of whether God is able to guide you. It may be perplexity about whether he is interested in guiding you. It may be that your future is preying on your mind. You are a believer now, and that is great; but how will you fare later on? May you not prove to be like Demas, who 'loved this world' and deserted (2 Tim 4:9)? Or like those of whom John wrote: 'They went out from us, but they did not really belong to us' (1 Jn 2:19)? What if disaster struck your life or persecution arose? You feel that you would go under.

These are genuine problems, not in the least exceptional or uncommon. That is one reason why there are so many Bible verses that speak to them – for example:

Do you matter? 'Cast all your anxiety on him, because he cares for you' (1 Pet 5:7). Another translation could be: 'It matters to God about you.'

Is assurance possible? 'If God is for us, who can be [successfully] against us? I am convinced that [nothing] will be able to separate us from the love of God that is in Christ Jesus our Lord' (Rom 8:31, 38–39).

Is prayer worth it? 'In everything, by prayer and petition, with thanksgiving, present your requests to God' (Phil 4:6).

Will he lead? 'He guides me in paths of righteousness' (Ps 23:3).

Will I make it? 'Being confident of this, that he who began a good work in you will carry it on to completion until the day of Jesus Christ' (Phil 1:6).

Those are great verses, but God gives much more powerful help than isolated texts. Those texts, marvellous in themselves, are infinitely more glorious when seen for what they are: just some of the splendid details on the vast majestic picture that God has unveiled to us in the Bible. He wants us to stand back for a while and take in the whole canvas he has painted. He wants us to absorb and admire his breathtaking plan of salvation, the grand design of our Saviour-Sovereign. He wants us (to revert to the earlier illustration) to become familiar and thrilled with all the supplies he has laid on for our expedition. We will lose out if we merely run a cursory glance over this tin of food or that compass. Christ wants us to make our own all the resources he has bequeathed to us from his pioneering journey through life and death.

In the following chapters we stand, wondering in awe, before the immense, many-splendoured Bible picture of God and his purposes. Each chapter sets out some of the divine truths which our human minds need, and some of the heavenly resources which our earthly route will require.

They are not 'problem-solving' chapters, though they will, I think, answer lots of questions. But they do give wide-angle vision. They offer the framework of biblical understanding to enable us to see where our questions and problems fit in. They set up the base camp to equip and encourage us to go higher up and further on with God.

They will raise questions and that is all to the good. They did for those who heard this material when it was first given in a series in a local church. Some of the actual questions prompted by those addresses are given at the end of each chapter; and you may well find there the very questions that occur to you as you read on.

Insofar as these chapters reflect the Bible's approach, they can change us from being problem-centred to being God-centred. They can root out our obsession with short-term cures and set us on the road to long-term spiritual health. They can lift us from the valleys of our own (little?) troubles to the high ground of loving God and knowing his love poured out into our hearts by his Spirit (Rom 5:5). They can settle doubts and fears and put a new spring of assurance into our step and our service.

The truths set out here have been the inheritance and delight of believers down all the centuries. They have been rediscovered in each generation – they have to be, because they get obscured by the natural mind (which does not like them) and the devil (who hates them). They are not in the least new in themselves, though they are ever-new. They have made strong, Christ-centred Christians out of weak, self-centred mortals ever since the days when they were first revealed. By God's Spirit, they still have that power – and that is exciting for us today.

Yes, there is excitement in these pages, though it is not the froth and bubble variety that recedes when the tide of events goes out or disappears when our fun bubbles burst. It is the excitement of being chosen for the expedition, of setting out to climb the heights. It is what Paul felt when he wrote: 'But one thing I do: Forgetting what is behind and straining towards what is ahead, I press on towards the goal' (Phil 3:13–14). The future is still future and therefore unknown, though a new part of it arrives every day. None of us has yet climbed the peaks that lie ahead, whatever our past conquests. This is why we may not see at once the relevance to the expedition of everything the Leader has said or supplied. We may fail entirely to see the point of this instruction or that item. Some information may make no sense to us at all right now; we may think we know better. Some maps are too detailed, we think; some directions seem odd. Surely we could work out a better route? But all that he has said and provided will come into its own as we go on. When we finally arrive, we will know that all he gave was absolutely vital to our survival and wellbeing.

It is sometimes like that with truths about God and ourselves. We may think that some of the Bible's assertions are totally irrelevant: why must we bother with 'doctrine'? Why can't we leave that to the academics and get on with life? We may even think some Bible teaching to be thoroughly objectionable. At such times we simply recall who gave its teaching: it was the One, the only One, who knows the route – all its contours and crevasses, all its gorges and glaciers. He knows it for two reasons: he made it and he's travelled it. That is why his instructive word and the supplies of his grace give us 'everything we need for life and godliness' (2 Pet 1:3). It was God's Son who pioneered the steep ascent to heaven; we must keep close to him, to listen and learn.

The more familiar we are with what he has revealed, the more we shall enjoy the climb and the views. The more readily we use what the Pioneer has supplied, the better will he be honoured by our progress and the more exhilaration will we find as we walk in his steps. The more you tread the high places in company with the Son of God, the more you will look back to thank him that you too were chosen for good and that he met 'all your needs according to his glorious riches in Christ Jesus' (Phil 4:19).

This book, then, is about the God who 'is able to make all

grace abound to you, so that in all things at all times, having all that you need, you will abound in every good work' (2 Cor 9:8).

# *Walking Tall, Fallen Short*

*by*

Peter Lewis

A few years ago I was speaking at a series of 'convention meetings' in the historic town of Chester. One afternoon I visited one of its fine museums. I shall never forget being confronted with two exhibits, which then stood side by side. In a glass case there lay the complete skeleton of a Roman slave, whose body had been thrown down a deep well; it had been covered with the rubble of a fire, which had destroyed the 3rd-century hostelry where he had presumably worked for high-positioned Romans. As a slave his body had been possessed as a mere implement and in death it had been tossed aside as refuse. Next to this exhibit stood a Roman altar, dedicated to 'the divine emperor Augustus'! The contrast between the two was total: in the one man was degraded; in the other he was deified. Each extreme was an appalling evil in the world which God had made 'good' and for his glory. Each showed a total loss of understanding about man: who he was and what he was for.

The Christian understanding of man is redeemed from this grim confusion by God's revelation in holy Scripture. For Scripture is given to tell us not only about God, but also about men. Wherever the testimony of Scripture has been unknown or neglected or repudiated, man has lost not only the true knowledge of God but also the true knowledge of himself, his fellow men, his world and his society. The

Bible's doctrine of man is crucial because it is true to *life* – and not just to appearances. It stresses both the dignity of man and the sinfulness of man; it guides us away from the callous abuse of man at the one extreme and from a naive trust in man's 'better nature' at the other. We are to understand men and women so as to respect and pity them, love and withstand them, expose and entreat them. And we are to go to the Bible for this understanding.

If someone came up to you and said, 'Tell me, what is the Bible all about?', what would be your reply? I think a good many Christians might give the short answer: 'Well, the Bible is about God; it is God's word about himself.' Now no doubt that would be right as a short answer, but it would be wrong as a long one! The Bible is, to be sure, a profoundly God-centred book, but though it places God at the centre, it does not dismiss man to the periphery. It does not put God everywhere and man nowhere. Man, too, is the focus of attention. From Genesis to Revelation the Bible is a book which tells us quite as much about man as it does about God. It speaks of God over man and man before God; God and man estranged and at enmity with each other; and God in Christ reconciling the fallen world of man to himself.

Nothing is allowed to obscure this two-fold focus. The Bible does not tell us about other worlds (except heaven), because it is concerned with this world. It does not tell us much about angels, because it is more concerned about men and women. It does not even tell us a great deal about God in a way which abstracts him from human life and from his concern with us. Only in a certain way are we to 'forget about ourselves and concentrate on him'. We must never imagine that the Bible is a kind of 'tourists' guide to God'. It is, throughout, the story of God's mighty acts in redeeming and saving a lost race, recovering in man the full beauty of the image of God in which he was made.

Yet the biblical view of man is not unopposed in the world – even in our modern world. Our societies do not hire slaves and they do not worship emperors, but they do manipulate masses and exploit individuals. They do teach man to worship himself, to pay homage to his proud self-image, to serve his lusts and his ambitions, to rely upon himself, his own understanding and his own potential – as if there were no God above him to adore, or alongside him to thank, or before him to meet. Let us look more closely at some of these alternative views of man.

## 'Get God out of the picture' – the Marxist view of man

The Marxist position is one which we might label 'optimistic atheism'. The Marxist, of whatever shade, is absolutely certain that man can do without God. In fact, for him there is no god anyway, so man had better get on without him! He is so convinced about this that he says, first of all, that man has it within himself to make it on his own; and secondly, that he will *not* make it on his own if he has religion, because religion acts like an opiate and dulls his senses. Marx held that, if people's lives were always orientated around a non-existent God and a non-existent after-life, they would never get where they ought to get. Religion, he said, simply diverts attention from the matters in this world (the only world there is for man) that need to be put right. For man to achieve his destiny, he must orientate himself around himself. He must get God out of the picture entirely, become utterly absorbed with himself and explain this world purely in terms of man.

Marxism is man-centred, and makes everything rely on man. This 'optimistic atheism', moreover, is sure that man *will* make it on his own; not, however, by gradual evolution, but by revolution. If man can change his society, change the class system, change the politics, change the economics, change the ownership of wealth, change the circumstances, then he can flower in his being and make his own Garden of Eden without the inconvenience of God. Change these outward factors and you change man.

**'The universe is absurd' – the existentialist view of man**

A second view of man has an unfamiliar name (existentialist), but a very familiar appearance. It is still frequently to be seen on our television screens. Some will remember the weekly *Wednesday Play* on the BBC in Britain in the 1960s; it was often a typical example of existential philosophy. Even today many novels and TV plays, in their sophisticated ways, are saturated with the mentality of the existentialist. This view is basically that the universe is, quite simply, absurd. It is there by chance, it has no meaning, you have no reason to think that it actually exists in any meaningful way. The world makes no sense, life has no point to it at all. You cannot relate to it, you cannot be sure of anyone or anything around you or above you. You cannot try to define your society, as the old philosophers used to do. You cannot think about truth, because absolute truth does not exist; once you have got outside yourself, life is just a mirage, unreal. You cannot verify it.

The only thing you can do is to accept that life is pointless and meaningless and then heroically *assert yourself* by doing *something* – anything (be it considered moral or immoral, constructive or destructive, purposeful or aimless) – so that you and at least that something exist and make sense. Thus, by asserting yourself, you begin to exist after a fashion; and that is the sum and substance of your worth. You are going to die like everybody else, your life is not going to have any objective value, but at least you will have been heroic and authentic in your loneliness. You will have cried out against the pointlessness of it all.

That was the philosophy behind many of the old kitchen sink TV dramas. They were a comment on the emptiness and boredom of life (and were they boring!); they had no plot or purpose, no beginning, no middle, no end. That was their whole view on life. Many, moreover, had a pessimistic and dismal ending. Whereas the Marxist is an optimistic atheist, the existentialist, like Jean-Paul Sartre for instance, is a pessimistic atheist: there's no point in anything. It is perhaps a small sign that this outlook does not ring true, that every now and again sentimental plays or films appear, where they all do 'live happily ever after'. But, without God, sentimentalism is as baseless as existentialism.

## 'Man's reason is the key' – the humanist view of man

This leaves God out as decidedly as the other two views. Unlike Marxism, however, it does not explain man in terms of class and economics, nor does it prescribe revolution as the answer. Unlike existentialism it is not pessimistic, but believes that man's reason can produce meaning and values and progress. Humanism is not new. It was in the ascendancy in Victorian days among poets and politicians and scientists too. Poets like Alfred Lord Tennyson dreamed of the future 'Parliament of Man' and moralized on our latent power to climb 'on the stepping stones of our dead selves' to higher things. Men applied Darwin's theory of biological evolution to social progress and looked forward to man's continued progress and self-refinement, as he journeyed from the primaeval slime to the stars! All the talk here was of man's nobility, power and possibilities for good.

This did not leave God out as the other views did, but it did leave behind the true biblical doctrine of the Fall. Even many of the Victorian preachers erred here in the general euphoria, promising that the imminent 20th century would see the most wonderful flowering of all man's latent goodness. Man was turning the corner and everything seemed to prove it: Victorian expansionism, British colonialism, America conquering its west, the flowering of the arts, the advance of science, the banishment of superstition, the success of politics in peace and prosperity. In all this it was man's reason which was stressed as the key to the future – reason as the way forward, discussion as the solution to conflict, science as the path to fulfilment, education as the route to a better world. Man, Victorian man, would turn the key of reason and open the golden gate of the 20th-century paradise.

But the gateway was not golden and the paradise proved to be a wasteland of war and blighted hopes. The First World War, which devastated civilization, ended that whole humanist era of optimism. The shallow, romantic hopes of two generations lay dismembered among the corpses which littered the battlefields of Europe. Humanism was dead – or it would have been, if it had not been for the incorrigible pride of man and his determination to trust to his own resources and to organize his society without God. So it survives still, in forms both secular and religious, always known by the first article of its creed: 'I believe in man.'

## 'Man stands before God' – the Christian view of man

The Christian understanding of man is radically different from all these opposing positions. That is because it is entirely controlled by the crucial consideration of man's relation to God. We say that the only way for man to understand himself is by understanding his God. The great 16th-century reformer, John Calvin, who is very significant in regard to the church's recovery of the biblical doctrine of man, put it like this: 'Man never achieves a clear knowledge of himself until he has first looked upon God's face and then descends from contemplating him to scrutinise himself' (*Institutes of the Christian Religion* Vol. I, chapter 1:2; Westminster Press, 1977 edition).

We must start with God if we want to make sense of anything, including (and especially!) ourselves. That is why Christians listen to God to learn about themselves, their world and their society. And we can acquire God's wisdom in these matters, for we have a speaking God, personal and concerned, holy and loving, all-knowing and utterly trustworthy. His explanation of man's failure and his uncovering of man's sin are painful and embarrassing, yet they are also hopeful and purposeful, for they are part of the means by which he leads us to his glorious revelation: salvation by Jesus Christ his Son our Lord, in whom we have redemption, the forgiveness of our sins.

The Bible sets out to explain man at the very beginning. The early chapters of Genesis are still the best explanation of the human race and of man in the 1980s. Man began as a unique being and not merely a member of the animal kingdom evolving by chance. The Bible tells us that from the start man had a unique purpose under the heavens. He was given tremendous dignity, being made in the image of God: 'Let us make man in our image, in our likeness' (Gen 1:26). Man is still in the image of God; that has not ceased to exist in him. But it is fearfully marred and hideously distorted; sin has added to it, as well as subtracted from it; sometimes it is hardly recognizable. 'Yet,' said Calvin, 'some rays of God's glory are to be found in man.' Even fallen man is still in God's image (Gen 6:5; 9:6; 1 Cor 11:7; Jas 3:9) and therefore has immense value, dignity and significance.

It is out of this conviction that Christians have effectively transformed life for women in challenging their subject-status and abuse in the ancient world; for the weak and the ill in pioneering asylums and hospitals; for the aged and for the outcasts in society. Christianity, with its doctrine of man in the image of God, could never have condoned a caste system, a slave trade or a doctrine of racial inferiority. And while Christians too have often been children of their times and short-sighted and wrong-minded because of sin, yet it remains a towering fact of human history that Christianity has done more than its opponents (who are in some respects its products!) will ever give it credit for.

Man in sin is like an ancient temple which has fallen into decay and ruin. Even in the ruins there is a certain grandeur that wins respect. 'If it is like this now,' we think, 'what must it have been like in its original glory?' Fallen man is a majestic ruin. Or he might be compared to a crippled athlete. 'I remember him,' we say, 'when he was so strong and straight-backed, a fine figure with great strength and reserve, so fast. Now look at him, twisted, broken, bent, racked with a cough, eaten away by disease, incapable even of walking.' That is Christianity's diagnosis of man in himself, a very serious diagnosis; one which is urgently necessary for a man to know about. The Bible X-rays man and holds his trouble up to the light. His great trouble is his sin, and the true nature and character of sin is only seen when man in sin is shown in his relation to God. It is then, and only then, that we see sin as it really is – not as immaturity, not as social maladjustment, not even as selfishness or self-centredness merely – but as *rebellion* against God.

## What man is like now

What is man's present state, especially in relation to God?

### *He is hostile*

What does Scripture say about man as he is now, by nature, in relation to God? It says first and foremost that he is deeply *hostile* to God. Paul says that 'the sinful mind is hostile to God. It does not submit to God's law, nor can it do so. Those controlled by the sinful nature cannot please God' (Rom 8:7-8). We have here a very strong expression in the Greek which does not simply say man is 'hostile', but that he is 'hostility' against God. There is in man now, and that at the centre of his being, a real and thoroughgoing, even violent, enmity towards God. Nothing challenges him, nothing threatens him, nothing provokes a hostile reaction in him, like God in his holy demands and his unbearable approach!

Of course, man is a religious, worshipping being. Yet the devastating indictment of Romans 1 is that man is as much a rebel in his religion as he is in any other part of his life. Even there he sins, suppressing unpalatable truth about God, bringing God down in his imagination to the level of the rest of fallen creation and exchanging the truth of God for a lie (Rom 1:18, 23, 25). Thus he tries to 'tame' God and appease his own conscience. But where the real God is concerned, as distinct from his convenient idol or his toy god, his opposition is radical, his rebellion is exposed. When the true God is preached, he reacts in fury or contempt. When the holy God approaches, he runs away in horror. 'God-haters' is Paul's summary description of mankind in this regard (Rom 1:30). Statements do not come stronger than that!

In his first letter to the Corinthians the apostle writes in a searching exposure of man's bankruptcy in spiritual matters: 'The man without the Spirit does not accept the things that come from the Spirit of God, for they are foolishness to him and he cannot understand them, because they are spiritually discerned' (1 Cor 2:14). Elsewhere he locates the reasons for this and traces them to a two-fold source: the hardening of the sinner's heart from within (Eph 4:18) and the blinding of the sinner's eye by Satan at work in 'his' society (2 Cor 4:4). The effect is as profound as anything can be, for as a consequence: 'The mind of sinful man is death, but the mind controlled by the Spirit is life and peace' (Rom 8:6). Any life not 'controlled by the Spirit' – and consequently the life of every non-Christian – comes into the category of 'death'. Even in his virtue, even in his worship, even in the highest reaches of his understanding and the greatest achievement of his moral character, he is – 'death'!

*He is condemned in that hostility*

Although it is beyond the scope of this chapter to go into detail about the doctrine of wrath in God against sin, we need to know not only that man is hostile to God, but also that he is guilty and condemned in that hostility. His condemnation is not simply the inevitable outworking of some impersonal law, but the effect of a personal reaction in God: the wrath of God. God's wrath is a corollary of his holiness as much as his love. When confronted with purity, righteousness and obedience, God's character expresses itself in blessing; when confronted with impurity, rebellion or sin in any of its forms, it expresses itself in wrath. All Scripture unites in this testimony, without which we cannot have a proper understanding of

God. The Old Testament idea of wrath is not in fact crude, as is so often supposed, but rather is refined and sensitive, aware of the holiness of God and its implications. All told, there are more than twenty words in the Hebrew Old Testament to express God's wrath and over 580 references to it.

The recognition of God's personal and outgoing wrath against sin, and so against man in sin (for sin does not exist apart from moral agents), is just as clear in the New Testament in the teaching of Jesus and of Paul. The apostle makes it clear that because of sin, not only is man hostile to God, but God is hostile to man: 'The wrath of God is being revealed from heaven against all the godlessness and wickedness of men who suppress the truth by their wickedness' (Rom 1:18). The picture that follows is of wrath, not only as an attitude in God, not even as a strong revulsion in the heart of God, but as a movement from God. A revulsion expressing itself, a wrath which is, in the words of John Murray, 'dynamically, effectively operative in the world of men . . . proceeding from heaven, the throne of God' (*Epistle to the Romans,* Marshall Morgan and Scott, 1967). The wrath of God is operative in human history now and not just reserved for the endtime of present history, and its greatest penalty, short of death and immediate damnation, is the repudiation of men and women 'giving them up' to greater sin and greater condemnation (Rom 1:24, 26, 28).

That condemnation is clearly and finally exposed in the third chapter of Paul's letter to the Romans, where he shows with unsparing insight the depravity that characterizes all men, so that 'Jews and Gentiles alike are all under sin' (Rom 3:9-18) and concludes: 'Now we know that whatever the law says, it says to those who are under the law, so that every mouth may be silenced and the whole world held accountable to God' (Rom 3:19). Man in sin, man fallen, rebellious and depraved, is beyond self-redemption. He cannot rise to God's demands, he cannot atone for his past sins, he cannot justify himself (Rom 3:20).

*He is hopeless in 'good' works, dead in sin*

Every attempt to 'buy off' God's wrath and to earn his forgiveness is doomed to failure – and indeed to further condemnation. Natural religion can go a long way, especially since God is at work in *common grace* in every man, restraining sin and encouraging goodness. But this, as we shall see, is abused by man. He sees his human 'righteousness' not as unworthy before God, not even (inasmuch as it is really present), as something achieved in him by God. He sees it as something with which to placate God, something which will one day be an effective protest against his final condemnation, something which can even indebt God to him. So fallen man turns religious – for a shorter or longer period of time – and tries to put himself right with God.

Jesus was faced with one of the most 'cleaned-up' men of his generation: religious, sincere and self-controlled Nicodemus. Jesus for ever spells the doom of all natural religion, the religion of the unconverted man, when he says: 'I tell you the truth, unless a man is born of water and the Spirit, he cannot enter the kingdom of God. Flesh gives birth to flesh, but the Spirit gives birth to spirit' (Jn 3:5–6). 'Flesh' here means the nature of fallen man, the unconverted heart. Jesus is saying that such a man, however motivated or self-changed, can only produce a religion that is fleshly, unconverted, polluted and corrupt. Fallen man is beyond self-help, he needs help from the outside. He needs precisely the thing he most dreads: the approach and the entry into his inner being of the holy God. He needs to be born 'from above' (a better translation than born 'again'), for only what God does will be sufficient for God and only what God gives will be acceptable to God.

When God comes, however, he will devastate man's self-confidence, rip up man's self-image, exposing his sin and his helplessness in sin. The man controlled by the Spirit admits this, indeed he insists on declaring it, that God might have all the glory of his salvation. 'Apart from me,' Jesus says, 'you can do nothing' (Jn 15:5). 'I know,' responds Paul, 'that nothing good lives in me, that is, in my sinful nature' or 'flesh' (Rom 7:18). Already we can perhaps see the folly of supposing a kind of moral neutrality to man in his better moments. He never rises above himself. And where is he in himself in spiritual terms? The starkest answer to that is given in the second chapter of Paul's letter to the Ephesians. Yet grim as the picture painted is, it is precisely in locating the hope of man *outside* himself that the apostle reveals the good news of the grace of God:

> As for you, you were dead in your transgressions and sins, in which you used to live when you followed the ways of this world and of the ruler of the kingdom of the air, the spirit who is now at work in those who are disobedient. All of us also lived among them at one time, gratifying the cravings of our sinful nature and following its desires and thoughts. Like the rest, we were by nature objects of wrath. But because of his great love for us, God, who is rich in mercy, made us alive with Christ even when we were dead in transgressions – it is by grace you have been saved (Eph 2:1-5).

The picture of man – as not simply straying, not merely sick, but actually dead – could not be more extreme. Yet it precisely reflects his plight in sin. Moreover, the further image of a resurrection for man in the powerful grace of God is just as precisely suited to his need, for it is not enough to bring the gospel to man, man must be brought to the gospel, his heart must be changed to welcome 'the light of the knowledge of the glory of God in the face of Christ' (2 Cor 4:6). That is no easy matter, as we shall now see.

## How man responds when faced with the gospel

Man's profound antipathy towards God nowhere comes out more clearly than in his attitude to the truth of the gospel, when faced with its claims. As we saw earlier, fallen man is a great suppressor of the truth. In order that he might pacify his conscience and allay his fears, he does two things. First, he suppresses 'what may be known' about the true God (Rom 1:19) and then he replaces it with a religion of his own, one which may be more easily lived with. In Paul's words, 'They exchanged the truth of God for a lie' (Rom 1:25). Consequently, when we come to the sinner with a gospel truth, he measures it *against his lie*. And the lie wins for him every time, because if he is wrong in his religion, he is wrong everywhere – and that he will not admit! In Jesus's words: 'If then the light within you is darkness, how great is that darkness!' (Mt 6:23).

Man's religion is the greatest enemy of God's truth, for man's religion is his self-righteousness, his one way of escape from the desert of his sins. Tell a man he is a sinner in his beer and he will probably agree with you; tell him he is a sinner in his religion and he may well strike you! Paul continually found, when witnessing to his fellow Jews, that it was not their impiety which kept them from God, but their religion; not their sins, but their righteousness. Hence he writes sorrowfully: 'Since they did not know the righteousness that comes from God and sought to establish their own, they did not submit to God's righteousness' (Rom 10:3). God had found a way to justify them, by giving his Son to live the perfect life that they could never live, and to die the atoning death for their sins. God's own righteousness in Jesus Christ was offered to them in the gospel, but they would not have it at any cost. They were so pleased with their own law-keeping that they rejected the righteousness of God for the righteousness of man. The bankrupt is offered £1 million, but will not admit he is bankrupt! He forfeits the wealth he so desperately needs, in order to keep up the appearance of solvency and hide the truth. So man, when faced with the gospel, continues to suppress and reject the truth.

Paul was writing about his generation, but might well have been writing about ours. He said to the Corinthian Christians that the message of the cross was 'foolishness' to their contemporaries – not something complicated, but something contemptible:

> The message of the cross is foolishness to those who are perishing, but to us who are being saved it is the power of God. For since in the wisdom of God the world through its wisdom did not know him, God was pleased through the foolishness of what was preached to save those who believe (1 Cor 1:18, 21).

And what was it that was preached against all rival systems? One thing and one thing only: 'Jews demand miraculous signs and Greeks look for wisdom, but we preach Christ crucified: a stumbling block to Jews [for the cross was a place of cursing] and foolishness to Gentiles [for how could a crucified man be a Saviour?].' It was contemptible to them all, 'but to those whom God has called, both Jews and Greeks, Christ the power of God and the wisdom of God' (1 Cor 1:22-24).

We today are ourselves faced with precisely the same kind of response. Our neighbours say: 'Well, if there are miracles, why don't you do a few?' Or: 'If God's there, why doesn't he appear and do something to convince me?' Or, if they are more intellectual: 'What's all this talk about blood? It's immoral to condemn somebody else for another person's sins. Anyway, there can't be any connection between an execution 2,000 years ago and my marriage breaking up or my drink problem. It doesn't make sense.'

Under his protests, however, and under his reasoning, are the deeper reasons, as we have seen. Man is not kept from God by his intellectual integrity, but by his sin, his rebellious heart. We hear the modern 'Greek', the 'wise men' of the age who often say: 'If I become a Christian, I'll be committing intellectual suicide.' But underneath their abstract reasons are the actual reasons – pride, guilt, fear and a profound dislike for God. The reasons why men are not Christians are fundamentally always the same. It does not matter whether someone is illiterate or whether he has five doctorates.

## Man's need when faced with the gospel

Some people appear to have no problem here. Some people believe that man's only need is to hear the gospel. They say:

'Oh, if we can only get the gospel out to people, everything else will follow; people only need to know.' Just as if it were only necessary for God to do his part and then leave the rest to man. But we can surely see the shallowness of such an attitude and its superficial understanding of man in sin, man in rebellion. God's work is far from done when he has brought the word of truth to man. The great work then is to get it past his prejudices and into his mind, to take it through his resistance and into his heart. God does not wait upon man for such a work or he would wait for ever. Here, if anywhere, grace needs to work *in its own power*.

For man in sin, when faced with the gospel, is unable to understand it. He fails to see his need of such provision or indeed the relevance of the provision of the death and resurrection of Christ. These things, says Paul, are 'foolishness to him'. He 'cannot understand them, because they are spiritually discerned' (1 Cor 2:14) and he by nature is destitute of the Spirit of God at this level. Moreover, he is the possession of 'the god of this age' who 'has blinded the minds of unbelievers, so that they cannot see the light of the gospel' (2 Cor 4:4). Sin within, society around and Satan over all – these are the factors which strive furiously to keep the gospel out of the heart and mind of the natural man.

The idea that man is morally neutral in some way is completely contrary to the word God has given us about man in sin. That word does not allow that, given an influence contrary to the world's influence, given an alternative to his present life in darkness by the approach of light, he will surely receive the light and embrace the new influence. 'The light shines in the darkness,' writes John, 'but the darkness has not understood it' (Jn 1:5). Men are not morally neutral, says Jesus, they are in bondage to sin and need to be set free: 'Then you will know the truth, and the truth will set you free . . . I tell you the truth, everyone who sins is a slave to sin' (Jn 8:32, 34). The truth itself, that is, the power of God working with and in and by the truth, is alone able to deliver men. Grace works in its own power.

The most explicit statements of Jesus to this effect are found in John 6 and they deserve our particular attention, as they show Jesus's own understanding of his opponents and his inevitable rejection by a God-hating world. There, faced with the profound distrust of his critics, he clearly articulates the doctrine of man's moral or spiritual *inability:* '"Stop grumbling among yourselves," Jesus answered. "No-one can come to me unless the Father who sent me draws him"' (Jn 6:43–44).

Earlier he had spoken of this 'drawing', not as a general calling or an indiscriminate grace which always accompanied the preaching of the gospel, but as an effective power and a particular act of God confined to a particular class of persons: 'All that the Father gives me will come to me, and whoever comes to me I will never drive away' (Jn 6:37).

Later, upon finding many of his disciples about to desert him, and knowing their hearts and the utter insufficiency of mere moral influences, he repeated his earlier words: 'This is why I told you that no-one can come to me unless the Father has enabled him' (Jn 6:65).

Such teaching, repeatedly given in Scripture, has given rise in Protestant theology to the doctrine of man's inability to respond to the gospel as he should. *The Confession of Faith* of the 17th-century Westminster Divines defines the doctrine of man's inability and his need for God's grace to work sovereignly and in its own power thus:

> Man, by his fall into a state of sin, hath wholly lost all ability of will to any spiritual good accompanying salvation; so as a natural man, being altogether averse from that good, and dead in sin, is not able, by his own strength, to convert himself, or to prepare himself thereunto. (Chapter 9, *Of Free Will.*)

Now it is very important for us to stress the *moral* nature of this inability. It is not the inability of the wheelchair, but the inability of the will. A man confined to a wheelchair by a physical disability is helpless in a different way and is not responsible for his inability to walk or run. But this is a very particular inability and one which leaves a man wilful and responsible in that inability. It is a bondage of the will and as such is a wilful bondage. This is clear from Scripture, however difficult it may be in logic. Paul, writing to the Ephesian Christians of the Gentiles who lived 'in the futility of their thinking', said that they were 'darkened in their understanding and separated from the life of God because of the ignorance that is in them *due to the hardening of their hearts*' (Eph 4:17–18, italics mine). Jesus spoke of it when he said to the Pharisees: 'You *refuse* to come to me to have life' (Jn 5:40, italics mine). He also spoke of it when he wept over Jerusalem: 'How often I have longed to gather your children together . . . but *you were not willing*' (Mt 23:37, italics mine). The great 19th-century preacher, C. H. Spurgeon, used to say: 'All their cannots are will nots.' That is what leaves men guilty as well as helpless.

## The question of free will

It is here that we meet head-on the controversial question of free will. It is controversial partly because justice must be done to both sides of the matter. C. H. Spurgeon had a delightful way (and a considerable gift) of reducing difficult things to simple and memorable explanation. He says:

> It is a difficult task to show the meeting-place of the purpose of God and the free agency of man. One thing is quite clear, we ought not to deny either of them, for they are both facts. It is a fact that God has purposed all things both great and little; neither will anything happen but according to his eternal purpose and decree. It is also a sure and certain fact that often times events hang upon the choice of men. Now how these two things can both be true I cannot tell you; neither probably after long debate could the wisest men in heaven tell you, not even with the consistence of cherubim and seraphim . . . They are two facts that run side by side, like parallel lines . . . Can you not believe them both? And is not the space between them a very convenient place to kneel in, adoring and worshipping him whom you cannot understand? (Metropolitan Tabernacle, Vol. 39, p.169 )

Much unnecessary dispute would be avoided if we carefully defined the term 'free will' against the background of the clear New Testament teaching about man's bondage in sin. The true and proper doctrine of human freedom is that man is free to choose what he pleases – that is, he is free to do according to his *real* desire. In his *Systematic Theology* (Banner of Truth) Louis Berkhof puts it thus:

> There is a certain liberty that is the inalienable possession of the free agent, namely, the liberty to choose as he pleases, in full accord with the prevailing dispositions and tendencies of his soul. (Part 2, p.248.)

The importance of this definition is that the will is not abstracted from the rest of a man's nature as if it were an independent and sovereign faculty. Man's will is determined by his whole character, it is rooted in the heart. Hence the unregenerate man's will can never be neutral when his mind is 'hostile to God' (Rom 8:7) and his heart 'desperately wicked' (Jer 17:9).

A fine illustration of this is given in an article, 'Man's Will – Free yet Bound' by W. J. Chantry. He writes:

> In modern times we observe rockets fired so that they escape from earth's gravity. To accomplish this there is a great complex of electrical wires, all woven into one control centre, called in the U.S., 'Mission Control'. According to the Bible, the heart is the Mission Control of a man's life. The heart is the motivational complex of a man, the basic disposition, the entire bent of character, the moral inclination. The mind, emotions, desires and will are all wires which we observe; none is independent, but all are welded into a common circuit. If mission control is wired for evil, the will cannot make the rockets of life travel on the path of righteousness . . . 'Will' may be the button which launches the spacecraft. But the launching button does not determine the direction. (Article in *Banner of Truth* magazine.)

He concludes:

> [the will] cannot choose without consulting your intelligence,

> reflecting your feelings and taking account of your desires. You are free to be yourself. *The will cannot transform you into someone else* . . . Here is the tragic truth about man's will. While free from outward coercion, it is in a state of bondage.

Hence: 'Men are not sinners because they choose to sin; they choose to sin because they are sinners!'

## The answer of free grace

Everything we have seen so far ought to lead us to the conclusion that man's only hope is God, that in himself fallen man has no hope. His dignity is not his hope, for he is a ruined temple. His morality is not his hope, for even his righteous acts are like filthy rags (Is 64:6). His will is not his hope, for while free from outward compulsion, he is in a state of bondage within, self-made bondage, self-determined bondage, self-sustained bondage. The prison is his own nature, not God's decree. Now only God's initiative, power and provision in Christ Jesus can rescue man and raise him. And that initiative, which sent the Son into an unwelcoming world, has to bring the provision of his atonement and resurrection into an unwelcoming heart by the power of an irresistible grace. *That* is the extent of man's need and that is the extent of God's mercy. Hence Paul's devastating picture of man 'dead in transgressions and sin', in the second chapter of his letter to the Ephesians, changes dramatically as the light of the grace of God breaks into the scene:

> You were dead in your transgressions and sins . . . but because of his great love for us, God, who is rich in mercy, made us alive with Christ even when we were dead . . . For it is by grace you have been saved, through faith – and this not from yourselves, it is the gift of God – not by works, so that no-one can boast (Eph 2:1, 4-5, 8-9).

It is something of a red herring to protest that 'the gift of God', which is said to be not 'from yourselves', may in the Greek (as in the English!) refer not to 'faith' but 'salvation', for it should surely be clear from our study that we cannot look for saving faith from the unregenerate sinner. Faith – that is, true and saving faith – implies a cleared understanding (however small) of the things that come from God, a true desire for God in his holy love and lordship, and a heart which is out of love with sin, sorrowing for a godless life. Man by nature is now incapable of such a self-transformation. He cannot rise above himself.

Paul's whole point in these verses is, therefore, to show that God has done for the believer what the believer could not do for himself. Our first thoughts of him were from him before they were of him. The first gleams of understanding of the gospel were the advance guard of his invading Light. Our dawning faith and earliest repentance were his gifts of love before they were our responses of love:

> For who makes you different from anyone else? What do you have that you did not receive? And if you did receive it, why do you boast as though you did not? (1 Cor 4:7)

Paul's death and resurrection metaphor in the Ephesians passage is as final as anything can be: the dead have no initiating or co-operating part in their own resurrection. They move because they have been moved; they live because they have been given life; they are free because they have been released from an extreme bondage. Man can affirm his 'freedom' until he is blue in the face and cold in the grave, but what he needs is resurrection. And that is precisely what God brings to men and women in the effective working of the gospel.

This is why the historic Reformed creeds and canons have defended so strongly what are often called the doctrines of grace. It is not so much a case of defending party dogmas as defending and asserting the true nature of grace and the unassailable place it has in the theology of our redemption. God is rebuilding the ruined temple, God is restoring the crippled athlete, God is raising up from a graveyard world a living church, a Bride who will live for ever with the Husband who chose her, for: 'Where sin increased, grace increased all the more' (Rom 5:20).

## Some questions about human nature before God

Q: You referred to 'common' grace. What is this?

A: The old Reformed theologians, wishing to do justice to all God's acts and operations of goodness and mercy in the world and in the lives of fallen men and women, distinguished two kinds of grace in God's government of the world: his common grace and his saving grace.

*Saving grace* is the undeserved favour of God drawing the soul to himself. It is an effective work of his love, in which the Holy Spirit moves in the depths of the sinner's being, enlightening his mind, turning his will and changing his heart. It is a work which issues in the new birth. As its name implies it really is saving and as such it is confined to God's elect.

*Common grace* is the more general, indeed universal, work of God in this fallen world and in the minds, wills and hearts of sinful men and women, restraining sin, exciting 'goodness' (at a human level) and reaching men and women with the familiar blessings of daily and seasonal life. It is the outflow of God's decision to love his enemies, even the non-elect, and to send rain and sun 'on the righteous and the unrighteous' (Mt 5:45). Even Reformed theologians have differed on details here, however, and I refer you for more prolonged treatments (though at a quite popular level) to the theologies of W. G. T. Shedd and Louis Berkhof. Shedd I find quite outstandingly helpful and enjoyable.

Q: How is God revealing his wrath today? Is God's wrath a withdrawal of common grace or an actual pouring out of wrath?

A: It can be both. Many people are so conceited about their achievements and their morality ('I've never done this or that . . .') and then later they run off with their secretary or fiddle the accounts. God may indeed withdraw common grace as a penalty for sin and this abandons the sinner to new levels of transgression and condemnation. This is the picture in Romans 1, of course, and you have perhaps a similar instance of it in the hardening of Pharaoh's heart in chapter 9. God's wrath, however, is shown in many other ways – including violence, injustice, disaster, tragedy, sickness and death – in fact all the penalties of the Fall. These are still real enough in the world, *even as penalties*. It is not only Adam who was punished! Even the believers are afflicted to a degree (Ps 90:7–10, 15), though in their case the sting of wrath and the curse are taken away (1 Cor 15:56–57).

Q: How much should we make of common grace?

A: In understanding man and in understanding the ways of God, I think we should make much of it. If we do not we shall, for instance, be unable to explain the goodness that there clearly is in fallen men and women – and that will make us much less convincing in the sight of people with whom we try to reason and talk. We should show them that they are all debtors at every level to the God they deny or neglect. Moreover, if we do not understand the reality and place of common grace, we may well find ourselves handing the case over to the Catholics and the Liberals, who have an inadequate (but more palatable and popular!) view of the Fall.

This doctrine helps us also to recognize God's complete freedom from blame when men reject the gospel. In correspondence with his desire for the salvation of all men, God gives them his common grace; that alone would be sufficient to incline and enable them to respond to his offers of salvation, *if it were not resisted*. The depth of man's antipathy for God, however, means that it always is resisted (Acts 7:51-52). Common grace *in itself* is sufficient, but because of the hostility of man it is not now and in fact sufficient. Grace is given and only sin makes inadequate. W. G. T. Shedd goes so far as to say: 'If common grace should prevail over the sinner's resistance, it would be saving grace.' But God, as we shall see in the next chapter, is not obliged upon the refusal of the first grace to come again with the second. That he does so in the case of the elect is *his* freedom and *his* right!

# *Loved with Everlasting Love*

*by*

Peter Lewis

If ever a subject could make us bristle, this one could: the Bible's teaching on election! The very mention of it is enough to raise defences, prejudices and wagging fingers, as Christians argue their different positions. So why study it at all? I could suggest many reasons, but I mention only two. My first would be this, without apology: it is *a doctrine of Scripture*. It is in the whole of Scripture, not just in one or two obscure and odd verses. It is written large in our Old and New Testaments. It was given to ancient Israelites as it is to modern Christians. Moses, David, and Isaiah taught it; our Lord Jesus himself taught it; so did Paul and John and Peter. There is no dissenting voice on this in the whole of Scripture. If we are Bible believers, we neglect what the Bible says to our loss, especially on a subject which is so deep and which is such a high privilege to enter.

## A doctrine of love

A second reason is this: it is first and foremost *a doctrine of love*. We are all concerned with the love of God; its height and length, its depth and breadth. Here we will find riches of God's love that will astonish us, thrill us and move us to heights of praise and thanksgiving, gratitude and love. Some folk misconceive election and think it must be anti-love. The exact opposite is the case. Election is very much a doctrine of God's love to you and me. It tells us that he has loved us, that he loved us before we loved him, that we love him because he first loved us. It tells us that God knew us before we were born, that he cared for us, that we had significance with him from all eternity, that we were never lost in the crowd. This is vital for the Christian's self-understanding, to know his God and know what place he has in the heart of his God.

## A doctrine of freedom

Further, and most important of all, it is *a doctrine of the freedom of God*. Dr Carl Henry states: 'At the heart of the election doctrine throbs God's freedom.' With typical shrewdness and insight the great Reformed preacher, C. H. Spurgeon, said long ago:

> It is said by someone that men give free will to everyone but God, and speak as if God must be the slave of men. Aye, we believe that God has given to man a free will – *that* we do not deny; but we will have it that God has a free will also – and that, moreover, he has a right to exercise it and does exercise it. You do not believe that God can justly give to some men more grace than to others. Very well. Let us kneel down and pray together . . . You cry (concerning relatives and friends): 'Lord draw them, Lord break their hearts, renew their spirits.' Now I very heartily use this prayer, but how can you do it, if you think it unrighteous in the Lord to endow this people with more grace than he does the rest of the human race?

These alone are sufficient reasons for looking at this truth.

The next question is: how are we to approach such a profound subject? How do we swim in such deep waters? I suggest three answers.

### *Approach with humility*

The first is: *with humility*. We should listen to the voice of God about this, not man. It is helpful to remember that when we were governed by non-Christian or worldly thinking, we stumbled at every Bible doctrine. They all appeared as offensive as this one may still appear to some. We once were offended at the doctrine that we were sinners, lost and damned, that our righteousness was as filthy rags, that there was a hell before us and a Judge above us. There was a time when we were offended at the gospel of blood and sacrifice and cross and suffering. We objected to being told that we could not save ourselves and had to be saved by another and on his terms. But we learned, by the Holy Spirit's work, humbly to listen to what God had to say about our sin and need, and his way of redemption. In this matter of election therefore we need simply to recapture that early humility and be willing to sit at the feet of God.

*Approach with caution*

My second answer as to how we should handle these truths is: *with caution*. We must stick to the plain statements of Scripture and avoid any logical flights into the doctrine of predestination that take it further than the natural sense of Scripture. We must believe *all* that Scripture tells us, but not *more* than Scripture tells us. For instance, Scripture commits us to the doctrine of unconditional predestination to eternal life, but not to that of unconditional predestination unto eternal damnation. I do not believe Scripture shows a double predestination of this kind, in which the two things are equal – as though God simply decided that he would create some for heaven and some for hell. That is more than Scripture tells us and is, in my opinion, a quite monstrous idea. It is true that sometimes great theologians have attempted to press logic too far in safeguarding what they thought were the rights and glory of God. But we need caution, lest we go beyond Scripture into philosophy, into insoluble problems (like the origins of evil), into doctrines that are extravagant and repugnant, even if apparently logical.

If a man is saved it is because he has been elected in the love of God to this salvation, and if a man is lost it is not because God has predestined him to be lost, but because he has rejected the offered love and salvation of God in Jesus Christ. God is the cause of faith; man is the cause of unbelief. God does not work in the unbeliever 'to will and to do' what is sinful, as he works in the believer 'to will and to do' his good pleasure (Phil 2:13). In a manner quite inscrutable to us, his sovereignty is as complete over the one as it is over the other; yet it operates so differently that God is never the author of sin and never the cause of man's perdition. Salvation is all of God, damnation is all of man.[1]

Dr J. I. Packer writes in his book, *Evangelism and the Sovereignty of God* (IVP, pp 22-23):

> God's sovereignty and man's responsibility are taught side by side in the same Bible . . . It follows that they must be held together and not played off against each other. Man is a responsible moral agent, while he is divinely controlled; man is divinely controlled, while he is also a responsible moral agent.[2]

1. Reformed theology has consistently defined God's *rejection* in terms of his *reaction*. That is, God does not decree to reject anyone, except on the ground of their sin. Only on this basis are some 'prepared for destruction' (Rom 9:22). Hence the *Westminster Confession of Faith* defines predestination to eternal life as 'out of his [God's] mere free grace and love, without any foresight of faith or good works . . . or any other thing in the creature as conditions, or causes moving him thereunto' (Chp. 111, para. 5). But it is careful to avoid an *equal ultimacy* in the decrees of election and rejection, as if *both* proceed alike from God 'without any foresight . . . or any other thing in the creature . . . moving him thereunto'. 'Election to life' proceeds purely from God 'to the praise of his glorious grace'. However, in regard to the decree of reprobation, we read in the *Confession*: 'The rest of mankind, God was pleased, according to the unsearchable counsel of his own will . . . to pass by and to ordain them to dishonour and wrath *for their sin*, to the praise of his glorious justice.' The phrase 'for their sin' is crucial. The 'passing by' is the rejection of *fallen* beings, men and women considered (albeit long before the event) as having rejected God. They are rebels before they are rejected.

2. This is expressed in the famous words of the *Westminster Confession of Faith* in the chapter, 'Of God's eternal decrees': God from all eternity did, by the most wise and holy counsel of his own will, freely and unchangeably ordain whatsoever comes to pass: yet so as thereby neither is God the author of sin, nor is violence offered to the will of the creatures, nor is the liberty or contingency of second causes taken away, but rather established (Chp. 111, para. 1).

These things seem to contradict one another, but both are taught in Scripture and must be kept together. They do not contradict each other in God's wisdom, only in our limited minds. We ought not to be surprised when we find such mysteries in God's word, for the Creator is incomprehensible to his creatures. C. H. Spurgeon was once asked if he could reconcile these two truths to each other. 'I wouldn't try,' he replied. 'I never reconcile friends who haven't fallen out!'

*Approach with gratitude*

The third answer to the way in which we should tackle election is: *with gratitude*. We are looking at the most exalted gifts of the supreme majesty and mercy of God to the most unlikely and undeserving. To think that he should set his love on us! The Christian is bowled over by that, lost in wonder, love and praise. Listen again to C. H. Spurgeon, whose preaching, like his life, was fuller of the joy of salvation than most. Here is an extract from a sermon entitled, 'David dancing before the ark because of his election' (on 2 Sam 6:20–22):

> Dear brethren, there is great power in the truth of election when a man can grasp it, when he knows for himself, truthfully, and by indisputable evidence, that the Lord has chosen him, then he breaks forth in songs of divine adoration and praise: then is his heart lifted up, and he pays homage to God which others would not think of paying. Personally, I have overflowing joy in the doctrines of eternal, unchanging love. It is bliss to know that the Lord has chosen me . . . Election sets the soul on fire with enthusiastic delight in God. Certain doctrines would not make a mouse move one of its ears; but the grand old doctrines of grace stir our blood, quicken our pulse and fill our whole being with enthusiasm. (*Metropolitan Tabernacle Pulpit,* Vol. 34.)

With such feeling and doxology does Paul open his letter to the church at Ephesus: 'Praise be to the God and Father of our Lord Jesus Christ . . . for he chose us' (Eph 1:3–4). Gratitude!

Among the various historic definitions of this doctrine of election the one put forward by the Synod of Dort in the early 17th century is one of the best and is worthy of concentrated attention:

> Election is the unchangeable purpose of God, whereby, before the foundations of the world were laid, He elected from the whole human race that had fallen from its primaeval integrity into sin and destruction by its own fault, according to the most free good pleasure of His will, out of pure grace, a fixed number of men neither better nor worthier than others, but prostrate with the others in a common wretchedness, to salvation in Christ, whom he appointed mediator right from eternity and the head of all the elect and the foundation of salvation; and resolved to give him to save them and to call and bring them effectually into his own communion through His own word and Spirit . . . He decreed to present them with true faith in Himself, to justify and sanctify them, and at last, being powerfully protected in the communion of His Son, to glorify them, for a proof of His mercy and for the praise of his glorious grace.

Strictly speaking, election refers to the people and predestination to the destiny he maps out for them, but we shall use the various terms (including foreknowledge, choice, decree, etc.) as virtual synonyms for the same basic concept. Let us look now at Scripture, not merely from the standpoint of man and his opportunities, but from the standpoint of God and his *plan of salvation*.

## Predestination and Christ

Jesus Christ himself was predestined to come to this world, as the Old Testament predictions showed – the types, the prophecies, the sacrificial system and those remarkable and astonishing passages in Isaiah 53 and Psalm 22. Those Old Testament features leave no doubt that it was planned and ordained that Christ should come into the world to live and die as he did. Yet Peter tells us that the predestination of Christ goes back even beyond Old Testament days: 'He was chosen before the creation of the world, but was revealed in these last times for your sake' (1 Pet 1:20). Peter is referring to Christ in his capacity and office as mediator. He is referring to the plan that he should become the God-man, to live and die and rise again for us, to accomplish the work of our salvation and redemption. That, he says, was ordained. Christ was chosen before the creation of the world. P. T. Forsyth once put it in a startling phrase in his book *The Person and Place of Jesus Christ:* 'There was a Calvary above, the mother of it all!'

### *Christ's own consciousness*

That Christ was predestined is also clear in Jesus's own self-awareness. His consciousness that these things were planned and ordained for him comes over again and again:

> He then began to teach them that the Son of Man must suffer many things and be rejected by the elders, chief priests and teachers of the law, and that he must be killed and after three days rise again (Mk 8:31).

He lived his whole life under the 'must' of prophecy. He knew that 'it is written that the Son of Man must suffer much and be rejected' (Mk 9:12). In the Garden of Gethsemane he said:

> Do you think I cannot call on my Father, and he will at once put at my disposal more than twelve legions of angels? But how then would the Scriptures be fulfilled that say it must happen in this way? (Mt 26:53–54)

Or again:

> It is written: 'And he was numbered with the transgressors' [Is 53]; and I tell you that this must be fulfilled in me. Yes, what is written about me is reaching its fulfilment (Lk 22:37).

As he predicted his death, he said: 'Now my heart is troubled, and what shall I say? "Father, save me from this hour"? No, it was for this very reason I came to this hour' (Jn 12:27). After his resurrection he said the same:

He said to them, 'This is what I told you while I was still with you: Everything must be fulfilled that is written about in the Law of Moses, the Prophets and the Psalms' (Lk 24:44).

*The purpose and motive*

This indeed was the purpose and motive of the incarnation (Heb 2:14–15): Bethlehem was in order to Calvary, the child was born to die, the Son was decreed to come for that great purpose. Nothing could be plainer. His whole life was a predestined and conscious pilgrimage to the cross. Christ was predestined to come, and – deeper mystery still – predestined to die. Now, if this were the only fact we knew about this doctrine, it would still be fundamental for us all. It is a difficult doctrine, we may find it a riddle of a doctrine, and yet it is the key to so many other riddles. It shows us the greatest, freest person in the world being predestined to do his work.

To those who say that predestination makes men robots, we respond by asking: 'Was Jesus a robot?' Nobody was more ordained than he. He said that he could do nothing by himself, but only what he saw his Father doing (Jn 5:19). His whole life was a looking to the Father for his will. Nobody was more predetermined than Jesus in every word he spoke and every deed he did, but nobody was freer or more responsible, more decisive or more in command. Yet his predestination clearly extended to the darkest event in his life, to the most terrible deed ever done, to the greatest enormity sinful man could commit, to the foulest, most vicious, most horrific, most tragic and most perplexing act in the world – Calvary! That was ordained and Christ was predestined to it.

*No accident, no mere murder*

The Bible forbids us ever to imagine that the cross was just an accident, any more than it was merely a murder. It was a purposed sacrifice. It is not as though God somehow rescued something in the end out of what was never meant to be; it was always meant to be. In the first Christian sermon, one

Jew said to his fellow countrymen:

> Men of Israel, listen to this: Jesus of Nazareth was a man accredited by God to you by miracles, wonders and signs, which God did among you through him, as you yourselves know. This man was handed over to you by God's set purpose and foreknowledge; and you, with the help of wicked men, put him to death by nailing him to the cross. But God raised him . . . (Acts 2:22-24).

'Handed over by God's set purpose and foreknowledge'! Peter uses three terms: handed over by God, God's set purpose, and God's foreknowledge. That foreknowledge is not God looking down a telescope to see what will happen and then trying to juggle events around it to make it all come right in the end. God knows what is going to happen, because he has decreed *either* to do it *or* to permit it to be done. He is never the author of sin, yet he is in control of all things – including the fall, the corruption, the chaos *and* the cross.

The Bible never has God on the sidelines, looking to see what will happen outside himself; that is no Christian doctrine. This comes out vividly in a prayer meeting – not a theological dissertation, but a prayer and praise meeting for ordinary believers in the early church. Peter and John had been threatened by the Jewish authorities for preaching Christ, but then, with reluctance, were freed. All the believers responded to the news of their release with great joy. They raised their voices to their 'sovereign Lord' in prayer and praise, and in their prayer we hear them give utterance to this conviction:

> Indeed Herod and Pontius Pilate met together with the Gentiles and the people of Israel in this city to conspire against your holy servant Jesus, whom you anointed. They did what your power and will had decided beforehand should happen (Acts 4:27-28).

Can we see the point? They (out of malice) did what his power and will had decided before (out of sacrificial love) should happen. God is never taken by surprise. Calvary, though the most terrible thing that God ever did, was in his mind from the start.

*Astonishing love*

This makes his love astonishing; that he should create a world to be the scene of this terrible agony; that at the beginning of time he should contour a hill which would become Golgotha; that when he first said, 'Let there be light,' he should start a series of events that would lead to the darkness in which his Son cried out: 'My God, my God, why have you forsaken me?' (Mt 27:46). It adds a breathtaking dimension to the love of God, that he was so determined to give us life eternal that, knowing the cost of it, nothing could stop him doing it. You may protest: 'But if it was so decreed, how could Judas or anyone be blamed for it?' Again we are given only two answers to that: God's sovereignty and man's responsibility, without further resolution. Jesus, who was privy to the most secret counsels of his Father, even when in the flesh, simply says: 'The Son of Man will go as it has been decreed, but woe to that man who betrays him' (Lk 22:22).

God acted for reasons unutterably good; Caiaphas, Pilate, Judas and the crowd acted for reasons despicably bad. God 'so loved the world that he gave [even up to the cross] his only Son' (Jn 3:16). He 'gave him up for us all' (Rom 8:32). He 'presented him as a sacrifice of atonement' (Rom 3:25). *He did it*, says Paul repeatedly, in those passages, with the full co-operation and will of the Son. God – 'who works out everything in conformity with the purpose of his will' (Eph 1:11) – fathered the greatest act of self-sacrifice that ever was or will be. God sovereignly overruled the malice of men.

*Not merely made available*

But, and this too is a recurring refrain, God did not send his Son to perform an empty gesture or merely to make salvation available to all. Jesus's preaching brings out again and again that there were people whom the Father had given him from all eternity, who would – unfailingly and without exception – be drawn to him. His death would most certainly be effective for them because of his deliberate, pre-destined and infallible intention to save them. This is no human theory, but the statement of Jesus in John 6:37, (starting from verse 35 to get the sense):

> Then Jesus declared, 'I am the bread of life. He who comes to me will never go hungry, and he who believes in me will never be thirsty. But as I told you, you have seen me and still you do not believe. All that the Father gives me will come to me, and whoever comes to me I will never drive away. For I have come down from heaven not to do my will but to do the will of him who sent me. And this is the will of him who sent me, that I shall lose none of all that he has given me, but raise them up at the last day. For my Father's will is that everyone who looks to the Son and believes in him shall have eternal life, and I will raise him up at the last day' (Jn 6:35–40).

All the elements are there. Jesus is freely available ('he who comes . . .'). Men are responsible ('still you do not believe . . .'). God is sovereign ('All that the Father gives . . .'). Christ is central ('I will raise him up . . .'). Predestination is a glorious fact ('I shall lose none of all that he has given me').

If we want to see how this operates in the consciousness of Jesus, we have but to turn to John 17. Jesus is about to die a death which will infallibly secure the redemption of his church. 'I have revealed you to those whom you gave me out of the world. They were yours; you gave them to me and they have obeyed your word' (Jn 17:6). Again: 'I pray for them. I am not praying for the world, but for those you have given me, for they are yours' (Jn 17:9). 'The world' there means the unbelieving, hostile world. Or yet again the same themes recur:

> Father, I want those you have given me to be with me where I am, and to see my glory, the glory you have given me because you loved me before the creation of the world (Jn 17:24).

Jesus tells us that he was not predestined to bring us merely to a temporary decision, that may or may not last for the rest of our life, but right through to glory – nothing less. And to do this for all his people in the ongoing work of the gospel in all the succeeding centuries – for those who will believe in the future (Jn 17:20).

*The covenant of redemption*

In these passages Jesus refers to a pact, or covenant, in eternity between the Father and himself, an agreement in which all the elect were given to him to be his eternal possession. This has been called in Protestant theology the covenant of redemption (the *pactum salutis*). It is not to be confused with the covenant of grace. The covenant of grace was made with men, in time; the covenant of redemption was made between the Father, Son and Holy Spirit in eternity.

This piece of teaching is no mere abstract or irrelevant speculation. It roots the church's election in the *Trinitarian* love of God. (The reason the Holy Spirit is not explicitly referred to is simply to focus attention on the Son's capacity as mediator.)

It rests the doctrine of election on the unshakeable faithfulness of God, who is committed *within himself* to the final salvation of all the elect.

The 'pact' itself does not so much indicate a 'moment' of decision in God (for we are loved from eternity in Christ), as a *plane* of decision, a level of commitment and a unity of purpose within the Godhead. It is surely the ultimate antidote to dark and fearful feelings about this subject of election in the minds of Christians. You and I were the subjects of a loving and eager agreement between the Persons of the Godhead in eternity:

> Grace first inscribed my name
> In God's eternal book;
> 'Twas grace that gave me to the Lamb,
> Who all my sorrows took.
>
> *Philip Doddridge*

Predestination relates to Christ; it also relates to the believer.

## Predestination and the believer

Old Testament believers knew a good deal about this doctrine, for they had been told, and not just once: 'For you are a people holy to the Lord your God.' Holy means special, cut off, set apart for God. 'The Lord your God has chosen you out of all the peoples on the face of the earth to be his people, his treasured possessions' (Deut 7:6). God did not choose Egypt, Assyria or Greece, but he did choose Israel (Is 43:3–4). For thousands of years they were the only people in the world who had the saving light of the gospel in its Old Testament form.

In the Old Testament, however, election was not just for the nation. By obvious implication and also by clear examples and explicit statements, it was for individuals also. As the Puritan, Thomas Goodwin, points out in his massive exposition of Ephesians (1:1-2:11), expounding the words 'the great love wherewith he loved us':

> God in his love pitcheth upon persons. God doth not pitch upon propositions only; as to say, 'I will love him who believeth and save him' as those of the Arminian opinion hold. No, he pitcheth upon persons. And Christ died not for propositions only but for persons . . . He loved us nakedly; he loved *us* not *ours*. It was not for our faith, nor for anything in us, 'not of works' saith the Apostle; no, nor of faith neither. No, he pitcheth upon naked persons; he loves you, not yours. (*Works*, Vol. 2, p.151; Nicholl, 1861.)

God's choice of persons is as clear in both Old and New Testaments as his choice of a nation. Abraham, the father of all the believers, was sovereignly chosen, selected and called out from Ur of the Chaldeans (Gen 12:1). His line of believing descent started with Isaac and Jacob and ran right on into the new era of Christ. Paul makes it clear that this involved individuals from the start, that Jacob was chosen before he was born:

> Rebecca's children had one and the same father, our father Isaac. Yet, before the twins were born or had done anything good or

> bad – in order that God's purpose in election might stand: not by works but by him who calls – she was told 'The older will serve the younger.' Just as it is written: 'Jacob I loved, but Esau I hated' (Rom 9:10–13).

*Selected or passed over*

This *election* involves an element of *selection*. That is how Jacob was chosen and Esau was rejected. Now there is nothing unjust in that, any more than there was injustice in God rejecting Pharaoh and using him, even 'hardening his heart', to further the divine purposes. Both Esau and Pharaoh were clay in the hands of the Potter, as Paul says (Rom 9:21). But the human clay which God shaped and directed, passing over and ordaining to destruction (Rom 9:22), was *fallen* humanity; human nature in its sinful state; people whom God bore with great patience, despite their impenitence (Rom 9:22). Even Esau in the womb (like Jacob for that matter) is part of a fallen race, a sinful totality (see Ps 51:5).

When we grasp that important theological truth, we can perhaps understand C. H. Spurgeon's swift reply to someone who objected to the statement: 'Jacob have I loved but Esau I hated.' Spurgeon retorted: 'Yes, I too have difficulty with that text: but it is not quite your difficulty. My difficulty is not why God should hate Esau, but why he should love Jacob!' That is a good example of wisdom and *humility* before holy Scripture.

You will find, moreover, that not only are Abraham, Isaac and Jacob spoken of in this way, but other individuals also. Take Jeremiah:

> The word of the Lord came to me, saying, 'Before I formed you in the womb I knew you, before you were born I set you apart; I appointed you as prophet to the nations' (Jer 1:4–5).

Paul explains his own ministry in the echo of these words and in the same way: 'God, who set me apart from birth and called me by his grace, was pleased to reveal his Son in me so that I might preach him among the Gentiles' (Gal 1:15–16).

### *The great and the ordinary*

No one, however, should think that only the leading figures in the church of God are singled out like this with special love and purpose. The great passages on the doctrine of election in the New Testament are written to entire churches of believers (young and old, weak and strong), who can all draw confidence from the doctrine *and their part* in it (for example, Rom 8:28-30; Eph 1:3-14; 2 Thess 2:13-15; 1 Pet 1:1-5, 2:9). We shall have space to examine more closely only the first of these. It would be enough, even if there were no other! In the eighth chapter of his letter to the Romans Paul writes (to a church he had never met, but a church of believers who were, like him, 'loved by God and called to be saints'):

> And we know that in all things God works for the good of those who love him, who have been called according to his purpose. For those whom God foreknew he also predestined to be conformed to the likeness of his Son, that he might be the firstborn among many brothers. And those he predestined, he also called; those he called, he also justified; those he justified, he also glorified (Rom 8:28-30).

### *The golden chain*

This has been called the golden chain of salvation, and it is a pity that some are embarrassed or unwilling to wear it! Notice that its first link and its last are in eternity. It speaks of a love for each Christian man, woman and child which reaches from eternity past to eternity future. Notice too that it speaks of *individuals* throughout ('those') and the *same* individuals throughout. Notice above all that it ascribes their eternal salvation to God and to God alone. It is God who works for their good, it is 'his purpose' which ensures their effective calling; it is God who 'foreknew' them and it is he who predestines them, he who calls them, he who justifies them and he who glorifies them. Nothing is clearer or more clearly emphasized throughout the passage than the primary truth that God initiates, sustains and carries through to a triumphant completion the saving work of his grace. The fact that Paul employs throughout verse 30 a tense which is used to point to a past accomplished event (the Greek aorist tense), is meant to point out with dramatic force this glorious truth: that the future of believers is as certain as their present and that nothing in all creation will be able to separate them from the love of God that is in Christ Jesus their Lord.

No attempt should be made to reduce the force of this passage. People have tried to do this in various ways. It has been said that the word 'foreknow' – 'those God foreknew he also predestined' – refers to foreseen faith and repentance; and that God's election is not unconditional, but based on his foreknowledge of our faith. This is refutable from several points. First, the passage says nothing of the sort. God does, of course, know who will turn and believe, but only because he has purposed to give to them the grace of faith and repentance. As the previous chapter has shown, man by nature consistently rejects all God's calls to faith and repentance. Listen to C. H. Spurgeon again:

> It is further asserted that the Lord foreknew who would exercise repentance, who would believe in Jesus and who would persevere in a consistent life to the end. This is readily granted, but a reader must have pretty powerful magnifying spectacles before he will discover that sense in the text. Upon looking carefully at my Bible again I do not perceive such a statement. Where are those words which you have added, 'Whom he did foreknow to repent, to believe, and to persevere in grace'? . . . As I do not find those words there, begging your pardon, I do not believe in them. (*Metropolitan Tabernacle Pulpit*, Vol. 18, p.182, 1872.)

*What does foreknowledge mean?*

Furthermore, this word 'foreknowledge' is not at all meant to lead us to imagine God looking on or looking forward, passively, to see what men will do. Such a picture would be in total contradiction to the whole thrust of the passage which, as we have seen, speaks repeatedly of *God's* activity. The term 'foreknowledge' is, in fact, full of positive content, just like the other terms that follow it. It has a two-fold significance: foreordination and distinguishing love. God foreknows because he plans, he decrees, he determines. In the light of Acts 2:23 and 4:27-28 *foreknowledge is clearly on the basis of foreordination*. God knows believers because he plans them and their lives (Ps 139:15–16). But he plans them not merely out of power but also out of love. As Professor John Murray states in his commentary on Romans:

> Many times in Scripture 'know' has a pregnant meaning beyond that of mere recognition. It is used in a sense practically synonymous with 'love', to set regard upon, to know with peculiar interest, delight, affection and action (see Gen 18:19; Ps 1:6; Amos 3:2; Mt 7:23; 1 Jn 3:1, etc.). 'Whom he foreknew' means 'whom he set regard upon' or 'whom he knew from eternity with distinguishing affection and delight' and is virtually equivalent to 'whom he foreloved'. (op. cit., p. 317.)

It is of great importance to get this right in our minds if we are fully to appreciate the love of God. He has not loved us so incomparably and so effectively because of something he foresaw in us, but because of something free and wholly undeserved in him. As far as mere foresight was concerned, all he could see in us was rebellion, sin and stubborn unbelief. Hence, says Professor Murray of the Romans passage:

> It is not foresight of difference but the foreknowledge that makes the difference to exist, not a foresight that recognizes existence but the foreknowledge that determines existence. It is sovereign distinguishing love (ibid. p. 318).

No wonder then, that Dr Martyn Lloyd-Jones, in expounding this passage in his great 'Romans' series, says that this term 'foreknowledge' is 'the most important term of the five' that occur in verses 28–30 (*The Final Perseverance of the Saints*, p.233, Banner of Truth). 'Indeed,' he says later, 'there is very little difference between foreknowledge and predestination.' The particular force of the term, however, reminds us that it was 'in love' that he 'predestined us to be adopted as his sons through Jesus Christ' (Eph 1:4–5) (ibid. p.239).

A further serious warning against mis-using this word 'foreknowledge' is given by Professor Donald McLeod:

> The very meaning of election to salvation is that our obedience is the result (and therefore cannot be the cause) of the divine choice. Our first movements towards God are due to His grace: 'Except a man be born again he cannot see the kingdom of heaven' . . . 'unto you it is given to believe on him' . . . Election based on faith and repentance is nothing other than love earned by faith and repentance. And then grace is no more grace. (*Banner of Truth* magazine, April 1969.)

The 'golden chain' is golden in its every link, from foreknowledge in eternity past to glorification in eternity to come. Let those who are in Christ Jesus wear it with joy, knowing that their names were written in heaven (Lk 10:20) before the foundation of the world (Eph 1:4; Rev 17:8).

*A doctrine of comfort for the believer*

We should recognize already that this is not a doctrine to avoid, but rather to glory in. It is not given to frighten us or to make us feel insecure in our salvation, but rather the opposite. We need not doubt our election if we have believed on the Lord Jesus Christ, for (as John Calvin emphatically and repeatedly taught): 'Christ is the mirror of our election.' In him as our Saviour and Lord we see the irrefutable evidence of our election by God. No one who has trusted Jesus Christ as their Saviour and given themselves up to him to be their Lord should have their confidence eroded by this doctrine – but rather established. It is the supreme comfort and strength of any Christian who is tempted to fear that he or she might not endure to the end or might not hold out against so many doubts and pressures and failures.

Paul's entire use and application of this doctrine answers this anxiety, allays such fear and establishes more firmly than ever the confidence of the believer. 'What, then, shall we say in response to this?' he asks at the end of the Romans passage. 'If God is for us, who can be [effectively] against us?' (Rom 8:31). The majestic assurance of the ensuing verses to the end of the chapter, are the outflow of this doctrine. They lead to the climactic cry of verse 39, that nothing in all creation 'will be able to separate us from the love of God that is in Christ Jesus our Lord'. Indeed, it has been said that the entire section which follows (Rom 9-11) is an exposition of that very statement given in the face of apparent denials and discouragements.

Similarly, Paul opens his letter to the Ephesian Christians, young and old, unstable and mature, with the same doctrine as a universal ground of confidence and rejoicing. Everyone, he says, who is in Christ, every believer, has in Christ Jesus blessings from eternity to eternity. All the blessings of a full salvation have been purposed for us in the Father's decree, purchased for us in the Son's redemption and decisively and definitively applied to us in the Spirit's ministry:

> Praise be to the God and Father of our Lord Jesus Christ, who has blessed us in the heavenly realms with every spiritual blessing in Christ. For he chose us in him before the creation of the world to be holy and blameless in his sight. In love he predestined us to be adopted as his sons through Jesus Christ, in accordance with his pleasure and will . . . In him we were also chosen, having been predestined according to the plan of him who works out everything in conformity with the purpose of his will . . . And you also were included in Christ when you heard the word of truth, the gospel of your salvation. Having believed, you were marked in him with a seal, the promised Holy Spirit, who is a deposit guaranteeing our inheritance until the redemption of those who are God's possession – to the praise of his glory (Eph 1:3–5, 11, 13–14).

It is very interesting to notice that John Calvin kept within this perspective very firmly when expounding this great doctrine. He did not attempt to construct a system around election or the decrees of God. Indeed he did not *start* with this doctrine at all. Some have done exactly that. They have begun their thinking with the divine decrees and have worked logically from that. And they have, variously, produced iron-clad systems which failed to do justice to *all* Scripture. Calvin was too firm and fair a biblicist to do that. In his great work, *Institutes of the Christian Religion,* he proceeds like this. *Book One* is on the knowledge of God the Creator; *Book Two* is on the knowledge of God the Redeemer; *Book Three* is on how we receive the grace that Christ has won for us. It is only in *Book Three*, and towards the end of that book, that Calvin begins to expound this ancient doctrine of election – as a word of pastoral comfort! If we kept that perspective in mind we should be less likely to wrangle on so glorious a subject.

*A doctrine of direction for the believer*

We are elected, not only to be happy in heaven but also to be holy on earth. Again and again this is brought out in the apostolic writings. God is not merely concerned that we should be happy; he has ordained that we shall be holy, a holy people in the holy Son, a holy people for a holy God:

> For those God foreknew he also predestined to be conformed to the likeness of his Son (Rom 8:29).

> . . . from the beginning God chose you to be saved through the sanctifying work of the Spirit (2 Thess 2:13).

> . . . who have been chosen according to the foreknowledge of God the Father, by the sanctifying work of the Spirit, for obedience to Jesus Christ . . . (1 Pet 1:2).

> His divine power has given us everything we need for life and godliness (2 Pet 1:3).

All these statements, like many others, tell us that God has elected us both to the goal and also to the way to that goal. Election is meant to strengthen us for service, not relax us for idleness. Knowing our sure and certain destiny, we 'press on towards the goal to win the prize for which God has called' us (Phil 3:14), making our 'calling and election sure' (2 Pet 1:10) by remembering who we are (2 Pet 1:9) and developing the new life of the Spirit which is in us (2 Pet 1:5–8).

We may never abuse this doctrine of election by saying or

thinking: 'Well, I'm chosen to eternal life, therefore I can now live in sin with impunity.' The new man or woman in Christ cannot take up such an attitude. Indeed, such is our change of heart toward God that we long to be nearer and more like our Father. If we were to be offered a choice between, on the one hand, heaven with a life in sin and, on the other, heaven with a life of righteousness, we would not hesitate to choose the second every time. Only the carnal heart regrets its farewell to sin, only an unregenerate person wants salvation *and* sin. For all our failures and trespasses, we are at war with all ungodliness and long for the day of our perfection. There is not a true Christian alive who prizes the doctrine of election as if it allowed him to live in squalor and look forward to heaven.

C. H. Spurgeon must have felt his blood stir when he addressed himself to this point in one sermon:

> It is whispered by some that election is a licentious doctrine. Say it out loud and I will answer you . . . The men who have believed this doctrine have been the wide world over the most zealous, most earnest, most holy men . . . Never were men more heavenly-minded than the Puritans . . . When a man believes that he is chosen to be a king, therefore would it be a legitimate inference to draw from it – 'I am chosen to be a king, therefore I will be a beggar; I am chosen to sit upon a throne, therefore I will wear rags' . . . No! the man, knowing that a peculiar dignity has been put upon him by God, feels working in his bosom, a desire to live up to his dignity. 'God has loved me more than others,' says he, 'then will I love him more than others. He has put me above the rest of mankind by his sovereign grace; let me live above them: let me be more holy: let me be more eminent in grace than any of them' . . . I heard a man say once, 'Sir, if I believed that doctrine, I should live in sin.' My reply to him was this, 'I dare say *you* would! I dare say *you* would' . . . To a man that is renewed by grace, there is no doctrine that could make him love sin . . . Here is a lion roaring for its prey. I will change him into a lamb; and I defy you to make that lamb, by any doctrine, go and redden its lips with blood. It cannot do it – its nature is changed. (*New Park Street Pulpit*, Vol. 6, p.136, 1860.)

*A doctrine of mighty encouragement in evangelism and life*

The doctrine of election is as far removed as possible from being a hindrance to our evangelism. It is, rather, an effective spur to it. That is implicit in what Jesus said in his great shepherd and sheep discourse: 'I have other sheep that are not of this sheep pen. I must bring them also' (Jn 10:16). It is all planned. Nothing can prevent it. And we are chosen to bring it to pass! This truth gave Paul heart in Corinth, the Soho of the ancient world. He was feeling challenged by the darkness, so overburdened by it that he did not know whether he should stay there. But;

> One night the Lord spoke to Paul in a vision: 'Do not be afraid; keep on speaking, do not be silent. For I am with you, and no-one is going to attack and harm you, because I have many people in this city' (Acts 18:9-10).

They were not the Lord's people yet; they were still out in the world, maybe murderers, perjurers or homosexuals, in a terrible state.

Paul later said of the church he founded at Corinth: 'And that is what some of you were, but you were washed, you were sanctified' (1 Cor 6:11). At the time of his vision they were certainly not washed or sanctified. They were lost, right out of the world! But God said: 'Many of these are mine, my elect, though as yet uncalled. I know where they are, in the back streets of this city, in the sewers of this Soho, but I'm going to draw them. They will be trophies of my grace. So Paul, you stay on and don't be afraid, for I'll protect you.' We know what a harvest Paul reaped there. They may have been a problem church, but they were also a glorious church, the crown of rejoicing for him in the last day.

The same truth appears in Acts 13:48, 'When the Gentiles heard this, they were glad and honoured the word of the Lord; and all who were appointed for eternal life believed.' This is an encouragement to our evangelism. To imagine that everything depends on us or on the other person would drive us frantic. If it were up to us to grab enough people and shake them and cajole them; if it depended on the fervency of our prayers or the cogency of our arguments or the consistency of our love . . . who would be saved? We would be in a panic. But New Testament evangelism is not panic! If we follow the apostolic way, we will listen to the Spirit and we will get up in the morning and say: 'Lord, who today? Where today? How today?' True, we will evangelize indiscriminately. We will not be trying to pry into God's secret plans, for only 'The Lord knows those who are his' (2 Tim 2:19). But we will always be listening in case God has further guidance, further direction. We will know that, if our hearts and lives are right, we need not be frantic; the Lord will fulfil his will through us.

This is a doctrine of encouragement in our whole lives, as well as our work and witness. The doctrine of God's decrees, his predestination of events and places, people and things, time and circumstance may terrify the non-Christian who is at war with God, but it should not terrify us. Where else would we like our life to be, but in the hands of our Father? Is there anyone else whom we would prefer to have sovereignty over every part of our life? Would *you* like to have sovereignty over your own life? I would not over mine. Horatius Bonar wrote in one of his fine hymns:

> I dare not choose my way,
> I would not if I might;
> Choose thou for me my God,
> So shall I choose aright.

Even the non-Calvinistic Christian is constrained to say that. As Joseph Parker's hymn puts it:

> God holds the key to all unknown,
> And I am glad;
> If other hands should hold the key,
> Or if he trusted it to me,
> I might be sad.
>
> What if tomorrow's cares were here
> Without its rest,
> I'd rather he unlocked the day

And as the hours swing open, say,
*'My will is best.'*

## Predestination and the churches

The doctrine of election is no sectarian or 'party' doctrine. It has been the age-old teaching of the Christian church and an awe-inspiring line of her greatest theologians have stood forth to teach and to defend it. Sometimes they have had to defend it from attack and dilution within the church itself.

The mighty Augustine expounded it against the humanism of Pelagius. Anselm and Aquinas wrote in its defence. Martin Luther wrote of it in his book *The Bondage of the Will,* against the humanism of Erasmus. The 16th and 17th century Calvinists, the Reformers and the Puritans, preached it against the Arminians. George Whitefield, the revival leader in England, and Jonathan Edwards, the great theologian in New England, defended it against the attack of the Wesley brothers. It is largely to John Wesley, great man of God though he was, that we must attribute much of the disfavour into which the old 'doctrines of grace' fell among evangelicals of the past 200 years. Yet in the 19th century, notwithstanding, William Carey and the Baptist Missionary Society, the Church Missionary Society and its earliest promoters, C. H. Spurgeon and his outstanding preaching ministry, were all products of (call it what you will) the old Augustinian, Reformed, Calvinistic theology of grace. Now, in the second half of the 20th century, we are seeing a recovery of the old apostolic doctrines of grace. In Britain this has been outstandingly through the pulpit ministry of the late Dr Martyn Lloyd-Jones and his published sermons on Romans and Ephesians (Banner of Truth). A new generation of evangelicals have rediscovered their roots and uncovered the foundations of their apostolic faith.

There has been a widespread unanimity about it in the great *Confessions of Faith* of the historic denominations. The *Thirty-nine Articles* of the Church of England say:

> Predestination to life is the everlasting purpose of God whereby before the foundations of the world were laid, he has constantly decreed, by his counsel, secret to us, to deliver from curse and damnation those whom he has chosen in Christ out of mankind and to bring them by Christ to everlasting salvation (Article 17).

In the Puritan *Westminster Confession of Faith* of the Presbyterian churches the introduction on 'God's eternal decree' reads:

> God from all eternity did, by the most wise and holy counsel of his own will, freely and unchangeably ordain whatsoever comes to pass, yet so as thereby neither is God the author of sin nor is violence offered to the will of the creatures, nor is the liberty or contingency of second causes taken away, but rather established; . . . those of mankind that are predestined unto life God, before the foundation of the world was laid, according to his eternal and immutable purpose, and the secret counsel and good pleasure of his will, hath chosen in Christ, unto everlasting glory out of his mere free grace and love, without any foresight of faith or good works or perseverance in either of them or any other thing in the creature as conditions or causes moving him thereunto, and all to the praise of his glorious grace.

The *1689 Baptist Confession of Faith* says:

> By the decree of God for the manifestation of His glory, some men and angels are predestined or fore-ordained to eternal life through Jesus Christ, others being left to act in their sin to their just condemnation.

There is a great unity in the historic Confessions and we may feel ourselves to be part of that unity. Our generation is very arrogant intellectually. People seem to think that other ages, former generations, knew nothing. That conceit sometimes can spill over into the church. Christians today can fall into the trap of believing that now they alone have got it together. We must sit, rather, at the feet of age-old teachers, not only the Calvins, the Luthers and the Augustines, but the Pauls and Johns and Peters, the Isaiahs and Jeremiahs. Through and with them, we must sit at the feet of the One who said: 'I have loved you with an everlasting love; I have drawn you with loving-kindness' (Jer 31:3):

Loved with everlasting love,
Led by grace that love to know,
Spirit, breathing from above,
*Thou hast taught me, it is so.*

## Some questions about election

Q: Do you need to know the exact moment when you became a Christian in order to know that you are elect?

A: No. One person, who did not know the day on which she was saved, had often worried about it. Then she came to see these truths and said: 'Now that I know that I was chosen before the foundation of the world, the exact moment of conscious experience does not seem to matter.'

Our present trust in Christ's finished work testifies daily to our election. We do not need to remember the day we were born to know that we are alive.

Q: 'I will have mercy on whom I have mercy' (Rom 9:15) seems to conflict with what Scripture says elsewhere about God's free offers of grace. Who has the ultimate choice?

A: God does and his choice is this: he has chosen not to take 'No' for an answer from his people who are among a race who all said 'No', and whom he knew would keep on saying 'No' until they were in hell and beyond. In that sense, he alone makes the ultimate decision.

Q: What does it mean when it speaks of God hardening Pharaoh's heart (Rom 9:18)?

A: It means what it says. It is clear, first of all, that we are not looking at a neutral Pharaoh, any more than we are dealing with a neutral human race. When God is said to 'harden' (either here, or in Isaiah 6, or elsewhere), he envisages man as rebellious, his human heart as *already* hard. And he is judicially 'giving him up', withdrawing his 'common grace' and leaving the sinner unrestrained in sin as in Romans 1. His hardening is not arbitrary, but judicial: a judge's response to a hardness already there. The sinner in question has abandoned all rights and has made himself liable to all sorts of penalty.

So Paul's answer is his abrupt: 'Who are you to reply against God?' If God does it, it must be right. And God does it in the context of enduring wrong, of being patient with the men ('the just and the unjust') on whom he sends his good gifts of the rain and the sun. All these explanations put the responsibility and the fault of damnation firmly on the shoulders of the sinner, not on the shoulders of God.

Q: Is it a waste of time to pray for people who are not elect?

A: We do not know who the elect are, so we have to go by what God tells us to do. He says: 'Pray.' That is how he gets things done on earth, through his people praying and speaking. I can, therefore, pray with complete confidence that this is what God wants me to do. I do not need to know if the people are elect. I know, on the basis of what God has said, that the chosen method by which he brings people in is by prayer and preaching. Often, when he lays in our paths people who seem interested, it is part of his sovereign working to lead us to pray and so to bring them in. The Lord has destined not only those who will be saved, but also the *means* by which they will be saved. If the Lord lays someone on your heart, that means God may be working in them – and you can pray with even greater expectancy for them.

Q: How does this truth of election relate to our praying for non-Christians?

A: We are commanded to pray for all kinds of men, and can pray for everybody we have ever met or shall meet. Prayer is never wasted, even if the answer is 'No'. First of all, the good of it comes back to us. Secondly, God himself, as old Thomas Goodwin the Puritan, put it, 'keeps it on a file' and may answer it years later. The Puritans who were ejected in 1662 prayed (Oh, those 2,000, how they could pray!) and prayed and prayed for twenty or thirty years, and then died in obscurity. But those prayers were not lost; the great revival under John Wesley and George Whitefield was the result of those prayers. That great outpouring was, in a sense, the outpouring of those great Puritan prayers.

When we come to praying for the unbeliever, we should indeed pray indiscriminately, but also we should learn to pray with a listening ear. Being 'burdened', being moved or guided in prayer is not to be treated lightly. If anything is 'laid on your heart', then you should follow it through. And if, when you are praying, you get a sense of victory in that prayer, then you are understanding the old saying: 'Prayer is the footfall of the divine decree.' The first hint you have of God's secret plan is there in that quiet assurance: 'It is going to happen! I'm sure it's going to happen!' Prayer is an adventure and it is exciting – never wasted, always purposeful. So we should seek guidance in our prayers, to be in line with the will of God.

A woman came to the church I serve whose parents had been godly people. They had prayed for her all her life until they died. Then, fourteen years later, she was converted. God had stored up those prayers in his heart and then poured out his answer 'in the day of his power'.

Q: Can somebody who is not among the elect be saved?

A: The previous chapter contains the answer to that. God knows that apart from election no one will ever receive his offer of life. That is because of the strength of man's opposition to God. The unconverted man is at enmity with God and those who are in the flesh cannot please God (Rom 8:7–8). The natural man cannot understand spiritual things because they are spiritually discerned; they make no sense to him (1 Cor 2:14). The God of this world has blinded their minds (2 Cor 4:4). They are darkened in their understanding, due to their hardness of heart (2 Tim 4:17–18). Always the element of responsibility is emphasized. But the inevitability of their negative reaction is obvious; there is no way in which salvation is welcomed, despite all the overtures and encouragements of God.

That was the state of the Jerusalem over which Jesus wept: 'I have longed . . . but you were not willing!' (Lk 13:34). Yet John 10:16 perhaps allows us to add as his thought: 'I knew you wouldn't, so now I've chosen sheep from all over the world, to bring them to myself.' This is God refusing to be defeated by the depravity of man. When the real gospel is presented to a person, he is outraged by it, he rejects it: it is 'a stumbling block to Jews and foolishness to Gentiles' (1 Cor 1:23). God's response in the case of the non-elect is to leave them (reluctantly and sadly) to their will in the matter. They do, as we saw in the previous chapter, receive grace, but they resist it effectively. That indeed is true of the elect also. But in their case God chose to 'come again', as it were, with the special power of an irresistible grace, which would not take 'No' for an answer. (That will be the subject of chapter four.)

Q: I have heard that since God is in eternity and not time, past, present and future have no meaning with him and that therefore this whole matter is irrelevant and all controversy needless. How would you reply to this?

A: The attempts to oppose time and eternity in this way have been pretty well exploded by some contemporary theological scholarship. Oscar Cullman wrote a celebrated book *Christ and Time* in which he defended the notion that God's eternity must be expressed in terms of 'endless time'. G. C. Berkhouwer, in his book *The Return of Christ* (pp.40–45), has similarly attacked the notion that we shall leave time behind when, after death, we enter eternity.

Where you have creatureliness, he says, you will always have time. Time, in fact, is not opposite to eternity, nor is time neutralized by eternity. The famous phrase in Revelation (probably more famous because of a popular Victorian song than anything else), 'time shall be no more', ought most properly to be translated 'there shall be no delay' (rather like our familiar saying: 'time has run out'). The fact is that for God too Calvary is 'past'; for God too the promises, like the decrees, have been irrevocably made; and for God too the glorification of the church is future: determined, desired and certain to be achieved.

# *A Death to Abolish Death*

*by*
Roy Clements

Moses died at the age of 120 and the Bible tells us that when he died he was as strong as ever. Buddha died at the age of eighty in peaceful serenity. Right to the end he had been surrounded by a great host of devotees who had been won over to his philosophy. Confucius died at the age of seventy-two. He had had setbacks in his early life, but at the end returned to his home town of Lu and had a great company of noble disciples there to continue his work. Muhammad died at the age of sixty-two, having thoroughly enjoyed the last years of his life as the political ruler of a united Arabia. He passed away, so we are told, in his harem at Mecca in the arms of his favourite wife.

You will sometimes hear people say that the origin of all religions is basically the same. They are all the creation of men of great intellect and spirituality. As the result of their reflection, they each discover some universal religious truth and then spend their lives teaching that truth to others. Eventually they succeed in producing an entire culture round that new insight. As far as Judaism, Buddhism, Confucianism or Islam are concerned, there is obviously a good element of truth in that opinion. All those religions were founded by people who died in ripe old age, having spent their lives teaching what they held. They died amid vast popular acclaim, with the future of their movements guaranteed.

In the whole spectrum of world religions only one is radically different: Christianity. Jesus died at the age of thirty-three, after a teaching ministry of three years at the most. He was ostracized by his own society, betrayed and denied by his own small circle of supporters, mocked by his opponents, forsaken – even by God himself.

He suffered one of the most ignominious and agonizing forms of public execution ever devised by human imagination. The founder of Christianity did not die in ripe old age, after a lifetime of teaching amid wide popular acclaim. His death was premature, tragic, lonely, on a cross, despised and rejected by man – a man of sorrows and familiar with suffering.

## How on earth?

The big puzzle is this: how on earth did a man, who ended his life amid such shame and ridicule, become the founder of the most influential world religion of all? The wonder of this is obscured for us, because we come 2,000 years after; we are used to thinking of the cross as a specifically religious symbol with a certain amount of holiness surrounding it. It has even become an item of jewellery to wear around our necks or an emblem to adorn our church buildings.

In Jesus's own day it was anything but religious or beautiful. It was repulsive, ignominious and offensive. The great Roman orator, Cicero said that the very name of the cross should never come near the body of a Roman citizen: it should not even enter his thoughts, his sight or his hearing. Yet the early Christians not only admitted that their founder had died in this contemptible manner, they boasted about it. 'May I never boast except in the cross of our Lord Jesus Christ,' said the apostle (Gal 6:14). 'We preach Christ crucified,' said the early church, though it is 'a stumbling block to Jews and foolishness to Gentiles.' To them it was 'the power of God and the wisdom of God' (1 Cor 1:23-24).

What possible significance, then, could that bizarre and

shocking death have assumed for them, that turned it from being an unmentionable infamy to a badge of honour? How did the symbol of criminal execution come to adorn Christian buildings and even Christian people? And why? Why did Jesus die? No single question is more important than that. The third chapter of Paul's letter to the Romans gets us off to a good start in answering that question by showing us that it had to do with sin, with human moral failure, and with total depravity. In chapter 3 he says: 'For all have sinned and fall short of the glory of God, and are justified freely by his grace through the redemption that came by Christ Jesus' (Rom 3: 23–24).

## 'Of course he'll pardon me!'

Many people make a great mistake at this point – people who know a little bit about Christianity, but not enough. They think that it is easy for God to forgive sins: 'Of course he'll pardon me, that's his business.'

But it is not as straightforward as that and it is crucial to see why it isn't. The explanation is all tied up with a phrase that comes several times in Romans 3, but particularly in verse 21: 'a righteousness from God'. Now *we* can forgive with no difficulty at all, because we are guilty. If we did not forgive people who sinned against us, it would be terrible hypocrisy.

For God it is quite different. First of all, he is morally perfect; that means that sin is a thousand times more offensive to him than it is to us. He is much more sensitive to it. Secondly, and even more importantly, God is the ground of all moral values in this universe. None of us is that, but he is. Take love, for instance.

Everybody agrees that love is better than hatred, but why do we believe that? Where does that moral value come from? What gives it substance? Is it just our emotional preference? Is it just a social convention that we have all accepted? Is it an instinct bred into us by our evolutionary origins? No. According to the Bible, love is better than hatred because God is love.

That is the root of it. It is God's moral character that guarantees moral values and makes them absolutes – things that are true for all of us, whether we agree with them or not.

We can overlook evil and it does not matter too much, but God is not like us. If God overlooks evil, it is as good as saying that evil does not matter – does not matter anywhere, does not matter in the universe at all.

That is an accusation which God cannot allow to pass unchallenged. Put in a single sentence, God's difficulty with forgiveness is this: how do you distinguish forgiveness from moral indifference?

If morality is to be preserved in the universe, it is absolutely necessary that God's righteousness should not only be done, but be seen to be done. In Paul's word, it needs to be 'demonstrated' (Rom 3:25-26). God must in some way dissociate himself personally from evil in the world. He must make a clear stand against it. If he does not, then all morality, standards and values are themselves undermined.

## In the role of judge

How can God do that? One very obvious way in which he can do that is to assume the role of judge. He can promulgate a law, defining the moral standards for which he stands. He can translate his own moral character into the imperative, into commands for us. He can then exact penalties from anyone who breaks those laws. That, according to the Bible, is precisely what God does. Under the terms of the old covenant, in the Old Testament, that is what he was doing in what we call the Ten Commandments. He was expressing his moral character in laws and saying that if people do not keep them, they will be punished. The trouble with that particular demonstration of God's righteousness is that it results in the universal condemnation of the world. As Paul says: 'There is no-one righteous . . . every mouth may be silenced and the whole world held accountable to God' as a result of this law (Rom 3:10, 19). As God casts his eyes around the universe, his verdict is: 'There is no-one righteous, not even one.' His demonstrated righteousness becomes his manifested wrath.

That is the central theme of the first three chapters of Romans. It is the difficulty, if we may put it this way, that God is under in seeking and planning to save the world. This sin problem is so deeply embedded in everybody, and the law cannot help.

## Any alternative?

Is there an alternative? Is it possible for God's moral character still to be asserted, his righteousness still to be demonstrated, but in some other way? Is it possible that instead of condemning human beings, his justice could actually acquit human beings? That seems impossible because we are guilty. How could God ever treat us as anything other than what we are? Yet Paul's astonishing news is that such an alternative is actually available. 'But now,' he says (notice these words in verse 21: they mark a line that separates history into two great epochs), 'but now' something dramatic has happened, as a result of which it is possible for God still to be fully righteous, and yet at the same time to declare human beings who are sinners righteous. He can be just *and* 'the one who justifies the man who has faith in Jesus' (3:26). 'There is,' he says, 'a righteousness from God apart from law'.

'Apart from law' does not mean that we can learn about it anywhere else except in the Bible. It means that the Bible does not contain this demonstration of God's justice in the same way that it contains the Ten Commandments.

It is not a matter of law. It is not a matter of God standing as judge against sinners. God adopts a different role in this demonstration of his justice.

The focus of this new demonstration of God's righteousness is Jesus. 'This righteousness from God,' he says, 'comes through faith in Jesus Christ to all who believe' (3:22).

This is the central answer we are looking for to the question: why is the death of Jesus so important?

Christians sometimes talk in a rather gory manner about the blood of Christ. And if we have had any knowledge at all of the Christian gospel, we know that blood has something to do with forgiveness, as it says in the children's hymn:

> He died that we might be forgiven,
> He died to make us good,
> That we might go at last to heaven,
> Saved by his precious blood.

Many people have some vague notion of that kind, but the vast majority even of Christian people, have little understanding of precisely how that death of Jesus is connected to forgiveness.

## A moral influence?

Many people try to interpret the death of Jesus as if it were just some kind of moral influence on us. That kind of interpretation of the death of Jesus goes back a long way in history, to a man called Peter Abelard. In the middle ages he was a considerable theologian. He said that the purpose of Jesus's death on the cross is to move us to love God. That is the way he saves us from our sins. He dies on the cross, he makes a great demonstration of God's love on the cross, and that moves us so much, emotionally, that we want to love God.

A man who came later had a similar theory. Socinius, the founder of the Unitarians, said that the death of Jesus was a moral example. It was the completion of Jesus's perfect obedience to the will of God. According to him, Christ saves us by revealing to us the way we ought to live; the cross, he said, is the final focus of that.

Whether people follow the line of moral influence with Abelard or of moral example with Socinius, they are saying something like this: that as we look at the cross, we feel conscience-stricken about our sin, we realize where we have been going wrong, and we determine to put our lives in order as a result. That is their theory of how the cross works. Christ's death becomes a kind of model of self-sacrificial love, that moves us to be better people or sets a great example to us.

There is a strong element of truth in the view that Christ's death has the power to move our emotions and to be a supreme example to us. Many people have been challenged by its dramatic power, by its exemplary power. There's no doubt about that. But such a view of the death of Jesus is open to major objections.

## Moral blackmail

First of all, take the moral influence theory of Peter Abelard. That savours of a particularly vicious form of moral blackmail. Do we really believe that God, faced with a morally rebellious world, would try to manipulate us with emotional levers?

To say that Jesus's death is a moral influence on us reduces his cross to the level of an IRA hunger strike. A hunger strike embarrasses the people who have to watch so much that they are manipulated into doing something – at least, that's the theory. It does not actually achieve anything: it is a gesture, some might even say a rather infantile gesture, certainly a purely histrionic gesture. It does not actually do anything, except to manipulate emotionally those who allow it to happen. It is a kind of moral blackmail. Can we seriously accept that that is what God was doing in Jesus?

## Totally irrational

Or take Socinius's view, that the death of Christ is a moral example. That is open to the charge of being totally irrational. Think of it this way. Imagine a boy and a girl, walking along a river bank, in love. The boy says to the girl: 'I love you and to show how much I love you, I'm going to jump into this river and drown.' The girl might be a little perplexed by that. I think the logic would not be transparent to her: 'All right, he loves me and he dies for me, but – well I don't quite see the connection. It doesn't make sense, it's irrational.'

In order to prove love, the loved one must benefit from the dying in some genuine way. It is no good anyone saying, 'I'm setting you an example of my love,' unless some benefit accrues to the loved one as a result of the dying.

If, however, the girl were in the water, drowning, and the boy said, 'I love her. I will dive in and rescue her,' that would make sense. Then we could see the connection between his risking his life and his love for her. Unless there is some clear benefit of that kind coming to that girl as a result of his dying, it is nonsense to talk about an example of love being there in the death.

It is the same with Jesus. Many people cannot understand the cross because in the terms of this illustration, they imagine Jesus walking along hand in hand with them on the river bank. 'Everything's nice in the world because God loves me and isn't it wonderful?' The Bible says the true picture is that we are in the water, perishing, and we need to be rescued. It is only because Christ came to achieve that rescue that we can speak of his death being 'loving'.

## Totally subjective

The problem with these views of moral influence or moral example is that they both touch only our feelings. They are totally subjective. They suggest that the purpose of the cross is to change our inward attitude to our sins, and so to move us to some kind of self-reform.

Now, whatever grain of truth about the cross there may be in that, what Paul is talking about in Romans 3 is totally opposite. He is saying there that the cross makes a difference – not to how *we* feel about our sin, but to how *God* feels about our sin.

The cross is not a means of influencing us subjectively or of setting us an example; it is an objective vindication of God's righteousness. He did it, he says, to demonstrate his justice. That is what was going on on the cross. God was demonstrating his justice, in a parallel way to how he demonstrates his justice when he punishes sinners in hell.

His moral indignation against sin *has* to be expressed somehow or else God would leave himself open to the charge of moral indifference. On the cross, instead of asserting his horror at sin by judging *us*, according to his law, God displays that same horror at sin by punishing Jesus in our place. That is what it is all about.

## Substitutionary sacrifice

It is this vital truth which Christian theologians have sought to preserve when they speak of the death of Christ as a 'substitutionary sacrifice'. It is not a totally adequate phrase. The cross of Christ has more to it than that; but if we do not grasp the meaning in that phrase, we have not even got to first base in understanding what the cross is about.

## Ransoming or redeeming

Three important word groups in the New Testament's teaching about the cross have this idea of substitutionary sacrifice in them. Paul uses two of them in Romans 3. The first word group is 'ransom' or 'redemption'. It occurs in verse 24: 'The redemption that came by Christ Jesus.' The background of that word group is the slave market. It describes a slave, who is released on payment of a price. The money paid for him is, as it were, a substitute for the slave. The man does not have a slave any longer, but he has money instead. So a cost is involved in finding a substitute to release that slave.

Mark 10:45 is an important verse in this connection, coming from the mouth of Jesus himself. It shows that Paul was not proposing his personal speculations in this area, but was taking his lead from Jesus's own understanding of his death. Jesus said: 'Whoever wants to be first must be slave of all. For even the Son of Man did not come to be served, but to serve [to be a slave], and to give his life as a ransom for [literally, *instead of*] many' (Mk 10:44–45). A ransom, a redemption-price, instead of many. That is the substitutionary idea. Here is a person who is enslaved; Christ comes as a suffering servant and gives his life instead of that person, so that he or she may go free. That is the meaning of redemption or ransom.

## Appeasing anger

Paul uses a second word group: 'propitiation' or 'sacrifice of atonement' (Rom 3:25). The idea is this: if somebody is angry and you appease their anger or avert it, you are said to have propitiated them. You have turned their anger away, so that you no longer feel the heat of it.

That is the force behind the word here. Paul says that God presented Jesus as a propitiation, someone who averts the wrath of God. The meaning is clearly that Christ, as a substitute, bore that wrath himself and so turned it away from us.

## Reconciling

The third word group is 'reconciliation' and comes from the area of personal relationships. If our enemy becomes our friend, he is said to have been reconciled to us. In 2 Corinthians 5:20-21, where Paul uses this language, it is clear that a costly substitution is involved in the reconciliation process. Paul says: 'We implore you on Christ's behalf: Be reconciled to God. God made him who had no sin to be sin for us, so that in him we might become the righteousness of God.' There is the exchange, the substitution.

Imagine two little boys learning to write at an old-style school. The teacher says: 'You must finish this script, you must copy out this writing, absolutely perfectly, no mistakes.' One boy does it perfectly – his script is immaculate.

The other boy has a few little problems: the pen nib does not work properly, he gets his sleeve in the ink, and by the time he has finished the whole thing is a mess. Before the teacher comes in, the boy with the perfect script gives it to the boy who messed his up, and says: 'Here, that's yours.' Then he takes the marred one out to the teacher as his own and receives the punishment.

That is a very simple picture, but that is what Paul says happened on the cross. There was an exchange. '[He] made him who had no sin to be sin for us, so that in him we might become the righteousness of God.' A substitution takes place, and it is on the basis of that substitution that God's anger is turned away from us, that we are redeemed from the slavery of our sin, and that we are bought from its consequences under God's judgement and made God's friends again.

The New Testament presents these three word groups to give us its perspective, from a number of angles, on the same essential truth: that there is a costly substitution going on in the cross, which liberates us from the consequences of our sin and brings us back into a relationship with God, as friend with friend.

## Rooted in the Old Testament: Isaiah 53

All those word groups have a fascinating and extensive Old Testament background. Three passages are particularly important. First, Isaiah 53, which is where Jesus found his model of the suffering servant. It is very important to realize that Jesus did not dream this up for himself; he learned it from the Scriptures and was being obedient to what the prophetic passages of the Old Testament taught of his role as Messiah. We hear Jesus say in the gospels: 'The Son of Man *must* be crucified', 'The Son of Man *must* suffer'; and it is this Old Testament passage which lies at the root of that 'must' – the necessity he felt about the cross.

The key verses here are Isaiah 53:4–6: 'He took up our

infirmities and carried our sorrows, yet we considered him stricken by God, smitten by him, and afflicted. But he was pierced for our transgressions, he was crushed for our iniquities; the punishment that brought us peace was upon him, and by his wounds we are healed. We all, like sheep, have gone astray, each of us has turned to his own way; and the Lord has laid on him the iniquity of us all.' The prophet was writing that in a situation where Israel was suffering a great deal and asking: 'Why is it happening?' He was looking into the future, to the coming of God's Messiah, and seeing that when Messiah came, people would be asking the same question: 'Why is he suffering? Surely God's Messiah ought to be a person of victory?' This is the paradox: he comes to be the costly substitute for his people's sins, and so he has to be a man of suffering. Isaiah saw that, as Jesus did too.

## The Passover: Exodus 12

A second important passage in the Old Testament is very influential on the New Testament's way of describing these facts: Exodus 12 on the Passover. After the Jews had been enslaved in Egypt, Moses performed a number of miracles at God's instruction to try to persuade Pharaoh to let them go. Pharaoh would not. Finally, the crunch came: the last plague was going to be particularly devastating. All the firstborn children were going to perish in a single night, when the angel of death swept through the land.

The key to this event is in verses 12 and 13: 'On that same night I will pass through Egypt and strike down every firstborn – both men and animals – and I will bring judgement on all the gods of Egypt; I am the LORD. The blood will be a sign for you on the houses where you are; and when I see the blood, I will pass over you. No destructive plague will touch you when I strike Egypt.' The blood there is the blood of a lamb; they were instructed to take and kill a lamb and to smear the blood on their doorposts, so that it would be a sign for them.

On the face of it, the Passover seems complicated. We might think that if God wanted to distinguish the fate of the Egyptians from that of the Israelites, he might do it in a straightforward way, on ethnic grounds. Why all this ritual – especially when God is omniscient and does not need a red mark on the doors to identify the houses of Jews?

The answer is that this is not a simple example of racial discrimination. The Jews could not escape the judicial execution that God had planned simply because they were Jews. That is the whole point, for in their own way they had been just as obstinate and unbelieving as anybody else in that land. God could be as justly angry with them as with the Egyptians. Yet, of course, they were his elect people, the ones to whom he had made the promise. How could God be faithful to those promises and yet wipe them out in the way that he was planning? If justice demanded that the Jews be punished too, surely there was no alternative but to include them in this appalling holocaust.

That is where the surprise comes in. That is where the experience of Passover develops the meaning of the words of the Old Testament and provides a searchlight on the New. God does not pretend that the Israelites are innocent; such a verdict would be contrary to truth. Neither does he issue some cheap, blanket decree of pardon that would make a mockery of his own righteousness. Instead, he makes a provision, which would avert the judgement when it fell, for any who had faith to appropriate it. 'Each man is to take a lamb for his family, one for each household (Ex 12:3) – but what difference did that lamb make?

It is not hard to see, once we imagine the situation as they experienced it. Inside every Egyptian home that morning there was a dead son; inside every Jewish home there was a dead lamb. What conclusion would they draw from that? The obvious one, surely, was that the lamb died in place of the son. The passage goes on to impress this, saying that there must be a precise equivalent between the number of families and the number of lambs. Why? Because each lamb represented that family's firstborn son; each lamb substituted for that family's firstborn son; each lamb bore the judicial penalty of death that night instead of that family's firstborn son.

Every surviving eldest Jewish boy could say that night, with indelible conviction: 'That lamb died for me.' When the angel of death came through, and saw the blood, it was a marker that in that home a death had *already* occurred and that God's justice had been satisfied as far as that family was concerned. It was not just an ethnic marker of the Jews. It was a marker of people who had taken God's word and believed it as far as the substitution of the lamb was concerned.

## The day of atonement: Leviticus 16

One more passage in the Old Testament is vital in this whole framework of substitution: Leviticus 16, about the Day of Atonement. This also is an Old Testament ritual of immense significance, because it was the one day in the year when the sins of the Jewish people were ceremonially taken away. The way it happened was this: the High Priest had to take the blood of an animal, to carry it inside the temple, inside the tabernacle as it was in the wilderness, into the Holy of Holies. That was the very dark place which no one could enter, except the High Priest once a year. There he had to sprinkle the blood of the animal on the Mercy Seat – the gold covering of the Ark, the big box where they kept the Ten Commandments, which was kept in that holy place. We may well wonder what all that ritual was about.

The key to it is to realize that the blood was sprinkled there, in the sanctuary which symbolized God's presence. It was taken into a place which nobody else could see. Even the High Priest would have had a hard job to see anything there, because the place was in almost total darkness. It had no windows in it, it was a place of deep mystery. That blood had to be sprinkled in God's presence. It is terribly important to realize that the blood was there for *God* to see. In fact, the same point is made in the Passover: 'When *I* see the blood . . .' (Ex 12:13).

This points to the fact that this blood is not working a subjective change in the people. It is not changing the way they feel about their sins. Maybe it is doing that as well, but that is not its principal purpose. The point of that blood is for *God* to see it, because it makes a difference to him. That is the purpose of the ritual. A death has occurred. Satisfaction to God's justice has been offered. Once again comes this thought of costly substitution – an animal having to die in order for God to be able to pardon his people.

Again and again throughout the Old Testament we find this idea of substitution. Again and again we find New Testament references to these three key things. The *suffering servant* of Isaiah occurs, for instance, in 1 Peter 2, as well as many other places. The *Passover lamb,* of course, is at the centre of the Lord's Supper. It was a Passover supper that Jesus celebrated when the holy communion began. He did not take a lamb from the table, as was happening in every other Jewish home, he took bread from the table and said: 'This is *my* body . . . this is *my* blood.' He offered himself to them as the Passover lamb. And the *Day of Atonement* occurs very much in the letter to the Hebrews, as the way into understanding the meaning of the death of Christ.

Whatever word group we take, whatever Old Testament passage we read, the New Testament homes in constantly on this thought: that the death of Jesus was a substitution which makes a difference to the way God sees our sins. Christ took on himself the damnation that was ours and suffered in our place.

## Why did Jesus shrink from the cross?

That, of course, is why Jesus shrank from the cross – an

observation that ought to strike us as most surprising. After all, many Christians have gone to their deaths singing hymns, rejoicing. Jesus went to his death in a state of gloom, despair and deep sorrow, spending a whole night before it immersed in depression about it all. 'My Father, if it is possible, may this cup be taken from me' (Mt 26:39). Was Jesus a worse Christian than some of his followers? Could he not die more happily? His death, however, was a different death. His was a death no Christian has to die, for what he saw when he looked in that cup was our sin.

One objection is always raised against this argument that the Bible's way of seeing the death of Jesus is as a substitution for sinners – namely, that it is unfair. Surely it is grossly unjust for God to take an innocent person and punish him for all the sins of all of us?

Think back to that illustration of the two boys learning to write. Maybe you thought: 'Well, I'd consider it very unjust if they did that to my son – punished him for another child's mistakes. It would be scandalously unjust.' That is a fair and strong point, but it has a weakness which is simply this: when we look at Jesus, we are not seeing a third party as far as God is concerned. There are not three parties, only two: God – and us. Jesus was God on the cross. God was not punishing somebody else. That is why it had to be Jesus. He could not take a perfect angel and place the sin of the world on him. He could not even look around for a perfect man and make him the sin-bearer of the world. That *would* have been unfair. What God is doing on the cross is bearing our sins *himself,* so that Paul can say: 'God was in Christ reconciling the world to himself.'

Take another illustration. Imagine a married couple. Their marriage is going through a bad time and the husband decides that he wants to leave home. One day he walks out on her and goes off to sow his wild oats. In six months' time he comes back again. There he is on the doorstep; he says to his wife: 'I'd like to come back. I've changed my mind. I want to come home.' Think yourself into that wife's position: how does she react?

It seems to me there are only three ways in which she can react. She can say: 'I never want to see you again. Get out of my life.' She could probably say that in all justice. It would be perfectly just for her to say: 'Get lost.' But if she really loved that man, I don't think she would say that, would she? She wants him back. So 'Get lost' might satisfy justice, but it doesn't satisfy her love.

A second possibility would be for her to say: 'Well, yes, come in if you want. What do I care whether you come in or not? It makes no difference to me.' I cannot hear her saying that, not if her love is real. It does make a difference to her, for she has been grossly offended by what has happened, has been torn to pieces by it. She cannot say that she is indifferent. If there were indifference, there would be no love. That leaves only one other option.

If there is to be reconciliation, the only way is if she says to that man standing on the doorstep: 'OK, you may come in. But you've got to realize how much you've hurt me.' Unless he realizes, deeply, how much he has hurt her by his sin against their marriage, there's no real possibility of reconciliation between them. No possibility of forgiveness. No possibility of beginning again. He must realize the seriousness of what he's done and how much it has wounded her.

## The agony of sin to a moral God

That is exactly what God is saying to us in the cross: 'Your sins hurt me. You want to know how much they hurt me? Look at the cross and you'll see.' On the cross we see the Godhead stripped open, we see demonstrated the agony which the sin of the world is to a moral God. He did this to *demonstrate* his justice. No one can say to God, when he forgives you and me: 'God, you're being morally indifferent, letting that person go free. You don't care about his sin, do you?' God points to the cross. He says: 'I do care. That's how much I care. It's true that, in my patience, I have left sins unpunished. But that mercy I exercise toward men and women doesn't impugn my justice, because I have demonstrated that justice to the shock of men and angels. I have come down among men and borne the punishment they deserved myself.'

That is why the cross is neither moral blackmail nor an irrational gesture. The cross is the place where God makes forgiveness, where he makes reconciliation, where he enables himself to be the justifier of sinful people.

God wants us to understand that the cross was an act of substitution on the part of Jesus for sinful men and women.

## For whom did he die?

Now to the crunch question. For whom did Christ die in that way? If we had been satisfied with the moral example or the moral influence theory of the cross, there would be no problem. We could say: 'He died for everybody, he sets everybody an example. He has his moral influence on everyone.' That is because those theories make it all subjective. We have seen, however, that that does not do justice to what the New Testament says. There is an objective benefit in the cross for men and women. He is a substitutionary sacrifice *for* men and women there, not just an influence in them or on them.

May we then affirm, 'Christ died for everybody,' when we are thinking about the substitutionary nature of the cross? We can quickly see that we cannot, for a very simple reason: hell is not empty. If Jesus died as a substitute for every man and woman in this world, God could not justly condemn any. He cannot and will not exact punishment for sin twice, which is what he would have to do if Christ took their punishment and then they had to suffer it as well. What kind of a universal redemption is it, if some are still in slavery? What kind of a universal propitiation is it, if some are still under God's wrath? What kind of a universal reconciliation is it, if some are still counted God's enemies?

That is our problem in arguing for a universal atonement or a universal death of Christ, once we have recognized its substitutionary character. The consequence of that is that everybody is actually saved – that is, universalism.

Yet the New Testament makes it clear that hell is not empty. Nice as it would be to say to the world, 'Hell *is* empty,' we may not.

## Two alternatives

What then are we to conclude? John Owen, in his famous book *The Death of Death in the Death of Christ,* points out that there are only two genuine alternatives. The first is that something is lacking in the death of Christ, which we human beings have to make up for ourselves. Those who succeed in making it up therefore go to heaven, and those who fail to make it up go to hell. That is why hell is not empty. Something is missing in the death of Christ, which human beings have to make up for themselves. If that is not right, we can come to only one other conclusion: namely, that in the intention and purpose of God, when he thought this all out before the foundation of the world, Jesus's death on the cross was a substitutionary sacrifice not for everybody, but for a particular company, those whom the Bible often calls his chosen or 'elect'.

It is only to the Bible that we can go for help in sorting out which of those two is right. Take the tenth chapter of John's Gospel, for example, verses 14 to 16: 'I am the good shepherd; I know my sheep and my sheep know me – just as the Father knows me and I know the Father – and I lay down my life for the sheep. I have other sheep that are not of this sheep pen. I must bring them also.'

Jesus is talking specifically about his death and who it is for. He says it is for his sheep. Who are his sheep? Everybody? Talking to some of the Jews there, he said (verse 26): 'You do not believe because you are not my sheep.' We need to notice which way round he puts it. He does not say: 'You are not my sheep because you do not believe.' He says: 'You do not believe because you are not my sheep. My sheep listen to my voice; I know them, and they follow me. I give them eternal life, and they shall never perish.' When he talks here about his sheep, Jesus is distinguishing between two groups of people before him – those who are in his flock, and those who are not. And he says: 'I lay down my life for my sheep.'

The New Testament never speaks of Jesus dying simply to make salvation *possible*. The New Testament speaks about Christ dying actually to *secure* salvation for God's people, for the church. Of course, there are any number of references where Christ's death is predicated of 'the world', or where we read that Christ died 'for all'. We must not deny or doubt that there are universal dimensions in the death of Christ. Sometimes, when that phrase is used, 'he died for all', the passage is stressing the fact that Christ died for all types of people, all races of people, all classes of people, as distinct from just the Jews – which is what a lot of them would instinctively have thought. He died for everyone – all nations.

Sometimes when the New Testament speaks of Christ dying for all or dying for the world, it is stressing the fact that there is no limit to the power of Christ's death to forgive – it is sufficient for all men. Even if it is not *applied* to all men, it is *sufficient* for them. However, it is the *design* that God had in the death of Jesus that we are talking about here, not the worth of Christ's sacrifice.

Sometimes when it talks about Christ dying for the world or for all men, the Bible is making the point that there is no limit on the free offer of the gospel. In a true sense God desires all men to be saved, just as in a true sense God desires all men to be perfectly righteous. But God does not always decree that which he prescribes. God prescribes the remedy of Christ's atoning work for everybody, but it is part of the mystery of his eternal purpose that he does not apply Christ's atoning work to everybody.

Sometimes when the Bible speaks about Christ's death for all or for the world, it is hinting to us that there is a cosmic significance in Jesus's death. The angels are involved. Nature is involved. The whole universe is involved in this death on the cross, not just us. It is much bigger than just ourselves. It involves the cosmos. But however we understand those references which speak of Christ dying for all or for the world, we cannot get away from those references where the death of Jesus is described as definite or particular. 'Particular redemption' or 'limited atonement' are valid attempts to describe the truth that Christ's work is effective for his sheep, his church. Perhaps they now sound too negative, even miserly, to do justice to the positive results of the cross. 'I gave my life a ransom for many', Christ says. Who are the 'many'? It is the 'many' of Isaiah 53 – God's people, God's elect.

## Not a popular truth

We cannot pretend that this is a popular truth. The whole idea of 'limited' atonement sounds narrow.

C. H. Spurgeon pointed out last century, however, that the people who actually limit the cross of Christ are not those who hold this view, but the other view. The Bible affirms that Christ's death made certain the salvation of a great company that no man can number. The other view is that Christ's death made salvation possible for everybody, but certain for nobody. In that case we have to imagine Jesus going up to heaven after he had died, wringing his hands in anxiety in case his death were all for nothing. If he had nobody specific in mind when he died, there was no certainty in what he did. In that case we destroy those two truths set out in the first two chapters here.

We can no longer talk about 'unconditional election', because this 'universal' view about the cross makes salvation conditional on something human beings add. We can no longer talk about 'total depravity', because man cannot be fully helpless, since there has to be this extra bit he makes up for himself in order to be saved. In fact we can no longer talk about assurance, because it is no longer a sufficient ground for my hope of heaven that Jesus died for me – according to this other view he died for many people who will perish, and I might be one of them.

## It makes a big difference

What we believe on all this is not a matter of splitting hairs. It makes a great difference to the way we witness or preach. When I present the gospel on the basis of a definite atonement I can offer an all-powerful Jesus, who has accomplished salvation for sinners and offers it to them. If I present a 'universal' gospel I can only (if I am consistent), preach a rather pathetic Jesus, who is knocking wistfully on the doors of men's hearts like a salesman. Instead of preaching a total abandonment of self and a repudiation of all form of human merit, I would have to tell people: 'Look Jesus has done a great deal, but you've got to do just this bit to make it work.' Instead of talking about 'being rescued' in and from a state of hopelessness, I would have to start talking about 'making a decision' and 'committing yourself', as if people have something to contribute to their own salvation.

That, of course, means that when they get to heaven, they can sit there with their hands in their pockets and say: 'Of course, you know why I'm up here, don't you? *I* believed, you see. Oh yes, Jesus did a tremendous lot. I'm not taking away from that. I wouldn't be here without him. But if I hadn't believed, I'd be down there with them. I did the extra bit. That's why I'm here.' In that case there would be boasting in heaven. We could feel a touch of pride – I believed, they didn't. That entirely misunderstands the nature of faith. It turns faith into a good thing we do, the merit of which earns us salvation. That is not the way the New Testament speaks about faith.

## The cross and our worship

There is a still more important aspect of all of this, however. The way we see the death of Jesus, whether as a particular redemption or not, makes a radical difference to our worship.

We began by seeing that Jesus's death has had a phenomenal impact. Moses, Buddha, Confucius, Muhammad – they were all great and admirable men, all of them. Why is Jesus's death so much more important than theirs?

It is all tied up with that verse: 'the Son of God, who loved me and gave himself for me' (Gal 2:20). It is because Christians down through the ages have been captivated by that – 'he loved *me* and gave himself for *me*' – that the death of Jesus has the power it does in our lives. Yet that kind of testimony is only possible if you see the death of Christ as directed in God's purposes not just to men in general, but to 'me' in particular.

## Questions on the death of Christ

Q: If God planned to save only a certain number, did he not fail? Did he not lose the rest to Satan?

A: The opposite is true. We can speak about God failing *only* if he intends or plans to do something, and fails to achieve it. We do not know why God did not plan to save everybody, but the Bible is clear that this is the case. If he had purposed the salvation of everybody and yet not all were saved, then he would have failed – the cross would have failed.

In fact, the view of the cross that sees Jesus as just making salvation *possible* – rather than as actually accomplishing it – opens up the possibility that it could have been a total failure, with no one saved at all. On that view we might all have said to God: 'No, thank you very much.' The truth is the other way round. We magnify the greatness of God in achieving his *purpose*. We may puzzle and wonder why his purpose was not different, and that is a dilemma; yet there is a limit to the type of questions we mortals may ask God. We may want to ask: 'Well, God, I understand what you purposed and I see you achieved it. But why didn't you purpose something else?' We may not ask such a question without being impertinent.

Q: The Bible says Christ died for sin, but did he die only for some sins (those of the elect) and leave out the others?

A: One very important dimension of the cross is that Jesus substituted himself for the sins of individual men and women. That is how God justifies them; he is able, without imperilling his own justice, to forgive those people, because his anger against their sins has been demonstrated against Jesus rather than against them. That is the effect, the logic of the cross. The substitutionary work of Jesus was for the sins – all the sins – of some men. Other sins were left out of that equation, the sins which take those outside Christ to hell.

Certainly there are some texts in the Bible which speak of Christ overcoming sin – as it were with a capital 'S' – sin almost personalized. The cross has cosmic dimensions in terms of conflict with Satan and overcoming Evil, with a capital 'E'. Those universal dimensions to the cross relate to Christ's conflict with Satan, Sin and Death. They do not obliterate this other, central dimension of the cross for us as individuals because the question is: whose side are we on, Christ's or Satan's, in that conflict? It is not Satan alone who falls under Christ's victory on the cross. It is everybody who is on his side.

The individual and the cosmic are not two conflicting models or ways of understanding the cross. When Christ dies as our substitute, he dies also as our victor over Satan. And he dies to build a new world from which Evil and Sin and Death will be excluded. There is an entire new universe implicit in what Christ has done. All agree on that, but it is those for whom he died as substitute who have a place in that new universe – not everybody without exception. So some sins are left out of that victory, the sins of those who are outside Christ, together with the devil and all his angels, who are punished in hell. That is the message of the book of Revelation: 'Christus victor' reigns with his saints.

Q: If some sins were not included in the atonement, was it really sufficient?

A: We must not confuse sufficiency with efficiency. To be absolutely accurate, some sins are excluded from the substitutionary *purpose* of God. Christ was not substituting himself for all the sins of all the world, or else everybody would be saved. Some sins are outside that substitutionary purpose. But the work of Christ's death is *sufficient*; had God purposed to save the world, he would not have had to have a second cross to make up enough atoning blood. The sufficiency is there to save the sins of the world, if God had so purposed. That brings us back to his purpose, but there is no doubt that Christ's blood was sufficient for all sin.

Q: How does John 3:16 (so loved the world) relate to election?

A: One difficulty is that we all come to this verse and understand 'world' in a universal, statistical, numerical sense – i.e. the world's population through all the centuries. We need to look at the way John uses the word 'world', because the term can have more than one meaning in Scripture. Sometimes it means the inhabited universe, sometimes this present age and its moral aversion to God.

So how is John using the word through his gospel? The basic meaning of it in John 3:16 (in Jim Packer's phrase) is: 'For God so loved bad men everywhere.' Christ came for bad men, sinners. He loved them everywhere, indiscriminately, regardless of class, education, money, language, previous religion or anything else. (Jesus is speaking there to Nicodemus, a member of the Jewish ruling council, and is making the point that it is not just Jews who will be saved.) He loved bad men everywhere in such a way that whoever believes in him will not perish, but have everlasting life. He is saying that something of value is available to bad men everywhere. Therefore we can go with confidence to a 'bad man' and tell him that, if he believes, he will be saved.

That does not take away from the fact that only those whom the Father gives will come to Jesus or that none can come unless he is drawn. This verse gives full justice to the universal element in the atonement, but homes in on those who believe. We can tell people to repent and believe in the full knowledge that sinners everywhere will come. John 3:16 defines God's love as actually *giving* life to those who would otherwise perish. Others, as verse 20 says, do evil and hate the light and *will* not come. God is benevolent to all, but love in the Calvary sense is love that actually saves.

Q: Does not 1 Timothy 2:6 seem to say that Christ Jesus gave himself as a ransom for *all* men?

A: In the earlier part of that chapter Paul is urging people to pray for all kinds of people (for kings and those in authority), that we may live peaceful and quiet lives. He is envisaging prayer for society. He wants it to be ordered in such a way that there is peace and order, so that (among other things) the church can function. He is thinking about all kinds of people; every type of person who makes up society. He is saying that we can confidently pray for all in authority, etc., because God ransoms all kinds of people (God obviously did not ransom all, or all would be in heaven). In this whole matter we do well to concentrate on the verbs – to save, to redeem, to give as a ransom, to be a sacrifice of atonement or to be a propitiation. They all mean what they say – that he saved, redeemed, etc., and did not merely make salvation possible. All the verbs used about atonement are definite; none of them says 'possibly', 'perhaps', 'maybe' . . . .

Q: Are we not in danger of trying to explain away a text like Romans 5:18 ('justification that brings life for all men')?

A: This verse sees a parallel between Adam (and death) and Christ (and life). Adam did not by sin provide the possibility of death; he brought it about. So Christ did not die merely to bring the possibility of salvation – he secured it. The problem is in the two words 'All' – all in Adam, all in Christ. If Paul means the same, universal 'All' in both parts of the verse, then we have to conclude that all men will be saved. In that case, the text proves too much, for clearly not all are saved. The only alternative is that when

Paul uses the word 'all' he is not speaking in terms of *all* men numerically, but of every type of person. Christ's death was not for one group out of humanity, in a social, financial, ethnic or educational sense, as a Jew might easily have thought. (When I say: 'Everyone come into the room for coffee', I do not mean the *whole* world! I have a particular setting in my mind. The same applies here.)

Q: What about the good shepherd who would leave the ninety-nine sheep in search of the one?

A: The point of that parable is that he *does* find the one. He does not just stand there wistfully wishing. He comes to 'seek and *save* the lost', not to seek and then make *possible* the salvation of those who are willing to co-operate.

Q: Is God unjust in punishing people and sending them to hell?

A: Not at all, because that is what all deserve. Paul asks and answers this very question in Romans 9:14. We labour under the liberal, humanist misconception that we are the measure of all things; we have to be humbled into realizing that we are creatures and that God does not owe us anything, even explanations. It is hard for us to bite that particular bullet, but that is what Paul is saying. We are creatures and God is God, the Creator. Indeed, God is magnified even in judgement. Far from seeing hell as God's failure, Paul sees hell as a triumph. It demonstrates God's righteousness (that evil is punished), even though the love of God has found another way to demonstrate it for his people.

Q: How does this affect our evangelism?

A: If I believe that Jesus's cross made up about ninety per cent of the way of salvation, and that anybody could be saved so long as they made up the additional ten per cent, I could never rest or have any peace. I would think: 'If only I could persuade them a bit better, if only I could manipulate them emotionally a bit more strongly, then maybe they'd make that ten per cent up and get saved.' I would be in a constant fever of anxiety as an evangelist, feeling that in the end it was all up to me. If I did not preach well, then people would go away saying: 'I'm not going to make up the ten per cent.' It would be all my fault for being such a pathetic preacher.

But thank God, that is not the way it is. My task as an evangelist (whether publicly or personally) is that of declaring to people the grounds on which they may come to salvation and assurance. I do this indiscriminately, *universally,* because that is what Jesus says I am to do – 'to all creation' (Mk 16:15). He does not tell me his secret plans. I do not know who is elect or who is not. He tells me to tell everybody and to declare to them that salvation is offered in this man, Jesus. When I see faith being generated under the word, when I see people coming to faith, I do not pat myself on the back, and say: 'That must have been a good sermon. You persuaded them really well there, Clements.' I say to myself: 'Thank God. Here is a sheep hearing the Master's voice.' That is what Jesus said: 'My sheep listen to my voice' (Jn 10:27).

When I see somebody else who turns a cold shoulder and walks away, I do not crumple up inside and say: 'It's all your fault, Clements, for being such a terrible preacher.' I will seek to love them and win them. But people walked away from Jesus, and he said to them: 'You are not of my sheep.' Those truths make that kind of difference; they give the Christian and the preacher genuine confidence. This is the only reason why a true evangelist in a hard place keeps going.

What if you believed that it was all up to you (or up to them), because 'you've got to persuade them'? If you were in a place like Arabia, where you never saw a convert for thirty years, you would give up, wouldn't you? You would say: 'This is hopeless. I'm never going to get anywhere.' We must remember how God spoke to Paul in Corinth: 'Keep on speaking . . . because I have many people in this city' (Acts 18:9-10).

That's the certainty, that's the logic: because God has got his people, preaching is bound to be effective, and we are on the winning side. There will be results, though they may take a long time to mature, though sometimes we will feel like Jeremiah, alone in the land. This confidence that God has his people will secure and encourage us, even when we may be going through a very unproductive period in terms of visible results. This is an incentive to evangelism.

Q: Why preach or witness, if the elect are going to be saved anyway?

A: The motive when we share the gospel is that they will be saved. But there's a higher motive: the glory of God. In no way is God more glorified in this world than through the salvation of his people, the accomplishment of the great pre-creation plan, the demonstration of his grace (Eph 1:6, 12-13). The extraordinary thing is that God has involved you and me in that purpose.

Paul does have a great desire for the lost (as in Romans 9:3), but what drove him to evangelism was not primarily the lostness of the lost. It was his wonder at the plan of salvation in Christ, and that he had been made a 'fellow-worker' in that. So he says: 'I planted the seed, Apollos watered it, but God made it grow' (1 Cor 3:6). That's the way he thought about evangelism. 'I and Apollos – we're nothing, but only God.' But if we do not believe that it is ultimately God who gives growth, we will become a mass of neuroses. We must be able to rest in the fact that 'I'm just a sower and waterer. You, God, give the growth.' I rest in that. I go to sleep at night, in spite of the fact that I'm deeply concerned for someone, because I know that God is the one who is in control.

# *An Offer You Can't Refuse*

*by*

Roy Clements

Why is it that some people manage to believe things that others find utterly incredible? In the upside-down world of *Alice through the Looking-Glass* it seems that faith is all a matter of effort. Lewis Carroll's White Queen says that you can believe anything, if only you try hard enough, if 'you hold your breath and shut your eyes'. But on this side of the looking-glass we, like Alice, know that it is not so simple.

There is all the difference in the world between faith and mere wishful thinking. To fail to observe such a distinction is to confuse reality with fantasy. Holding your breath and shutting your eyes is not to believe – it is to make-believe. And, by definition, anything you have to make yourself believe cannot be real. For reality constrains belief effortlessly. As Alice puts it, 'It's no use trying. One just *can't* believe impossible things.'

Yet, of course, Christians do. That is the mystery. Viewed in the cold, dispassionate light of reason, Christians believe in quite the most extraordinary things that it is possible to conceive – God coming down to live as a man. Alice could be excused for calling it impossible. Yet the Christian does not feel that he is *forcing* himself to believe it. He is not playing a game of 'let's pretend'. No self-hypnosis is involved. He believes under the constraint of what he feels to be the truth. How do Christians do it? It cannot be that they are just plain gullible. Some are pretty naive and credulous, but it won't wash to portray them *all* as dim-wits or dupes. No, there's an enigma here, the enigma of faith. Some people have it, others haven't. The question we must ask is: 'Why?'

John 6 sheds light on it. At the very end of this long discourse or conversation Jesus says: 'There are some of you who do not believe' (v. 64). Some people in that crowd listening to Jesus did not believe. On the other hand, Peter speaks on behalf of the disciples and says: 'We believe and know that you are the Holy One of God' (v. 69). So others there did believe. We must therefore seek the explanation for this division in Jesus's audience.

### Why this division?

It is not hard to find. Jesus tells us, not just once, but three times in this passage. He reiterates it in slightly different ways. First, he says: 'You have seen me and still you do not believe. All that the Father gives me will come to me' (vv. 36–37). Then: 'Stop grumbling among yourselves,' he says to these unbelievers. 'No-one can come to me unless the Father who sent me draws him' (vv. 43–44). Finally he adds: 'There are some of you who do not believe' (vv. 64–65). Jesus had known from the beginning which of them did not and would not believe, and who would betray him. He went on to say: 'This is why I told you that no-one can come to me unless the Father has enabled him' (v. 65).

Now those three statements of Jesus all set forth the teaching that theologians have called the doctrine of 'irresistible grace' or 'effectual calling'. Let me illustrate with a story I once heard from Dr Jim Packer (whose IVP paperback *Evangelism and the Sovereignty of God* I also strongly recommend).

### Head-first into the water

He tells of how, when he was a student in Oxford, he had once gone punting on the river – and had fallen head-first into the Thames. It was not, he said, a pleasant experience, because a mass of thick weeds entangled his legs and arms, and the water was very deep. For quite some time he was seriously afraid that he was going to drown; he just could not get to the river bank. He went on to imagine what his fellow students (who were safe and dry, still in the punt) might have said.

One might have said, as Packer gurgled away in the water: 'Oh, you'll be all right, Jim. You can get out if you want to. Just keep struggling.' A second might have said: 'Oh, I'd like to help you. But you see I've got this problem of conscience about interfering with anybody's free will. I can give you some tips about swimming if you like.'

Those two imagined reactions parallel two of the responses to Christ's work of salvation that history has thrown up. One is called Pelagianism, the other Arminianism – and they are both around today. Pelagians and Arminians both believe that the work of Jesus is very, very important; we cannot be saved without it. But they both also believe that if the work of Jesus is going to be effective in our lives, if it is going to be applied to us personally, then we have to make a little contribution of our own. The work of Jesus is not sufficient to save me on its own. I have to contribute something to get the work of Jesus out there on Calvary over here into my heart. And that contribution is *faith*.

## 'We all have the ability or the grace'

Pelagianism says that we all have the ability to believe in Christ's work of salvation if we want to, just by nature. Every human being has that natural ability. It is akin to the White Queen telling Alice: 'You can believe if only you practise a bit more. You've got it in you, Alice.'

Arminianism is slightly different. Arminianism agrees that we need supernatural help to respond to the gospel, but it says: 'God gives that help to everybody. It's just up to us whether we accept and use that help or not.' That is rather like the White Queen offering advice. Because God won't interfere with 'free will', he's still dependent on our *choosing* to respond to him. That is the element in both Arminianism and Pelagianism that we need to note. One way or the other, they are both saying: 'If you want to be saved, try harder. It is self-effort that will get you to the shore. You must choose, you must exert your will, you must try.'

That, however, leaves the question of what we do when, like poor Jim Packer, we're drowning and our strongest self-effort is not enough. As Alice says: 'It's no use *trying*. I can't believe impossible things.' What do you reply to someone who says to you: 'I'd like to be a Christian, but I just can't believe it'?

## An actual rescue

Packer pursues his illustration a little further. When he actually fell in the river, he was immensely glad that the people in the punt were neither Pelagians nor Arminians, but Calvinists. What actually happened was that a friend of his jumped into the river, overcame his helpless struggles, pulled him free of the reeds, brought him to shore, gave him artificial respiration – and put him back on his feet. 'That,' said Jim Packer, 'is what I call a rescue.'

According to John 6, that is what Jesus calls a rescue too. He is not content to say: 'Well, I'll do this much. But you've got to do that bit.' He is fully aware of the insuperable obstacles that prevent sinful men and women from believing on him as the bread of life. Yet he's not discouraged by that, because he knows that salvation is not a matter of self-effort – not ten per cent, not even one per cent. It is all a matter of grace, irresistible grace. This grace, he says, *draws* men and women; gently, with the wooing magnetism of a lover, not the brutality of a rapist (v. 44). It enables men and women to come to him, giving them what they need to engage with Christ, illuminating their minds to understand him, renewing their affections to love him, liberating their wills to move to him (v. 65). Grace, so that they do not have to make themselves believe, but embrace Christ by faith spontaneously, intuitively, effortlessly, irresistibly.

## 'I confess that God is God'

That, I suggest, is actually the way it happens. C. S. Lewis's autobiography *Surprised by Joy,* has a lovely section which speaks to my heart because it is very much the way in which I was converted. Lewis tells how he fought tooth and nail against the idea of becoming a Christian. But then, he says, there was one night when it all came to the crunch for him; he knelt down in his room at Magdalen College in Oxford: 'I confessed that God was God. At least,' he added, 'the Prodigal Son walked home on his own two feet. But who can admire that divine grace which welcomes a sinner, dragging him through the high gates of heaven, even when he's turning his eyes this way and that, looking for a way of escape?' Those words in the parable, 'Compel them to come in,' were sweet words to him, because that is how he experienced it. There was an irresistibility about God's grace.

Now we must be careful not to misunderstand the word 'irresistible'. We must not think that God coerces, brutalizes or dehumanizes us in the act of conversion. Quite the opposite. A moving incident in the Bible shows that this irresistible grace of God is gracious as well as being grace. It is the story of Lydia (Acts 16). She was a dealer in purple cloth, a business woman, a sophisticated lady from the city of Thyatira. We read: 'The Lord opened her heart to respond to Paul's message' (v. 14). Notice the gentleness of that description: 'He opened her heart.'

## Which side is the handle?

Evangelistic speakers ofter speak as if the door handle to our hearts were on the inside. They talk about *us* opening *our* hearts; it is not wrong to do that, in the sense that that is what it often *feels* like. But when Luke is inspired by the Holy Spirit to express it, he does not say: 'Lydia opened her heart' to respond to the gospel. He says: 'The Lord opened her heart.' That is the way round it is, for that is where the initiative really lies. The handle is on the outside and the Lord opens it. Our hearts are locked tight against the gospel by nature. It is not just that we do not want to open our hearts to Christ; we could not, even if we wanted to. 'No man can come to me,' said Jesus, 'unless the Father draws him.' Yet there is nothing brutal, nothing cruel, about this opening of the heart.

This is how C. H. Spurgeon put it:

> When you see a casket wrenched open, the hinges torn off, the clasp destroyed, then you discern at once the hand of a thief. But when you observe a casket deftly and smoothly opened, with a master key, you discern the hand of the owner.

In the same way, he says, conversion isn't a violent wrenching open of the heart, in which the will and the reason and the judgement are all ignored or crushed. God does not plunder human lives; that is the devil's way. God opens hearts, not like a beast his prey, but as the owner his own treasure. He comes to us as the Creator to his own creature and deals with the human heart according to its inner nature. God does not enslave the will, he frees it. He does not blind the reason, he enlightens it.

That is what we mean when we talk about irresistible grace or effectual calling. We mean that Jesus does not just abandon his work for us to accept or reject it as we will. He actually applies that work to men's hearts. This is the particular role of the Holy Spirit in the plan of salvation. God the Father planned the work of Salvation; Jesus the Son accomplished it; and it is the distinctive work of the Holy Spirit to apply it to our hearts, to make it real to us individually. And we must never, never steal that prerogative from the Holy Spirit.

**Is there an alternative?**

Obviously not all believers accept this teaching. There are real born-again Christians who (whether they know these titles or not) are Pelagians and Arminians. How do we relate to them? Is there an alternative to the teaching we have been setting out? I am a man whose heart is for gospel unity with all true born-again believers. However, God does want us to think things through biblically, while always rejoicing in the great truths we hold in common. And big issues are involved in this matter of grace that affect us and our churches very practically. We must each decide, in our own conscience and heart, with the help of the Holy Spirit, as we study the Scriptures, where we stand on these issues of grace. In particular, we must ask what happens if we take a Pelagian or an Arminian view of salvation.

The answer is, and it is a serious charge, that we thereby subtly resurrect a religion of works. Consider, for example, Paul's teaching in Ephesians 2:8–10:

> It is by grace you have been saved, through faith – and this not from yourselves, it is the gift of God – not by works, so that no-one can boast. For we are God's workmanship, created in Christ Jesus to do good works, which God prepared in advance for us to do.

What the apostle is saying there is that salvation is one hundred per cent grace – and that includes the faith through which we are saved, and the good works which follow from our salvation.

He is saying that the whole work is grace. You have been saved, totally, by grace. There's not an ounce of good works in it, and because of that there is not a single opportunity or excuse for boasting. Everything – the faith by which we appropriate salvation, and the good works that express it – are all God's workmanship, his creation, his deed. It is all by grace.

## We don't like charity

People, however, do not like such grace. They do not like charity, and for two reasons. First, because we're naturally cynical: we don't trust 'something for nothing'. The story goes that a man stood on Westminster Bridge, trying to sell golden sovereigns at a penny each. By the end of the day he had hardly sold any. Nobody believed that he was selling genuine golden sovereigns. We distrust charity. We feel there is a catch in it.

Secondly, because of our pride; we do not *want* charity. We want to be independent, to pay our own way. We don't like being put in a position where we owe anybody anything. Take Christmas cards: 'I'd better buy a few extra, because if somebody sends one to me and I haven't sent one to them, I shall have to get one off pronto, shan't I?' We don't want to be one down, we like to keep the score even. We want to 'pay' for what we get. We do not *trust* charity and we do not *like* charity.

That is why the history of the church has seen many people trying, one way or another, to twist the gospel to get the grace out of it, or to push the grace into a more acceptable shape. In Paul's own day such an attempt was made in the church by a group of legalists – people who played down grace and played up rules. They probably had their roots in the Jewish faith. They tried to say: 'Of course, the work of Jesus is great. But you have to add *your* contribution. You have to have circumcision, you have to have the works of the law. Jesus's work is fine, but it's not enough on its own – you've got to do your bit too.' Paul withstood that kind of legalism in the church very emphatically. 'The gospel is *free*,' he said. 'You do *not* contribute *any*thing. It is not of works.'

## After legalists, the sacramentalists

What Paul said on this point is so strong and clear that we might think that nobody would ever get it wrong again.

Sadly, it was not so. Once legalism had stopped threatening the church, a new kind of perversion crept in during the middle ages: sacramentalism. What the medieval Roman Catholic did was to say: 'Yes, of course, the grace of God is there. But how is it mediated to the individual? How does the individual get hold of the grace of God in Christ? He does so through the sacraments of the church.'

There were seven sacraments – baptism, confirmation, the mass, penance, holy orders, matrimony and extreme unction. Through these seven pathways the grace of God comes to you. And so you have a chance to do your bit. By coming to the mass, by going to confession and doing your penances, you make your contribution to getting hold of the grace of God and making it your own. It was not until a monk called Martin Luther stepped on to the scene that this particular heresy was broken – for heresy it is. The Roman Catholic church likens the sacraments to the veins of the body of Christ. Grace is a fluid that flows through this ecclesiastical plumbing to people.

That was how Martin Luther was brought up to think. He was a man of great sensitivity and moral conscience, not unlike the apostle Paul; and he was burdened with a sense of personal guilt. Being a good Catholic, he tried the sacraments, because the church told him: 'That's the way you get hold of the grace of God, that's the way you find forgiveness.' He tried them all. He went to mass regularly, he did penance until he was exhausted with it and had exhausted his confessors.

One day, in a thunderstorm, terrified by what he took to be the signs of God's judgement, he decided he would have to become a monk and he took up holy orders. But even that sacrament did not help him. He still felt burdered with his guilt. Only matrimony and extreme unction were left – and, as he had vowed monastic celibacy and was not dying, they were not available to him!

## Indulgences

Only one thing was left for him in the Catholic system – what are called indulgences. Indulgences, according to the Roman Catholic church, are special remissions of guilt, which the church has available to give. They are the result of the good works of all the saints down the centuries – their good deeds so outweighed their sins that they created a kind of moral surplus to share out. Indulgences were given on performance of certain special works of piety – such as giving money to build St Peter's in Rome, or going on a pilgrimage. Luther went out to obtain indulgences. He went on pilgrimage to Rome. He did all those things a true Catholic was supposed to do. At the end of it, he still knew he was guilty and hell-bound. The sacramental system had not worked.

Such additions to grace, such Pelagian or Arminian contributions, which you have to do to be saved – they never do help. All they finish up doing is to plunge people into a total lack of assurance. You can never feel saved if you're a legalist or a sacramentalist. You are always tormented by the thought: 'Have I done enough? Have I done it right?' The turning point of Martin Luther's life came when his father-confessor in the Augustinian priory told him that the only thing for him was to go to university and do a degree in biblical studies. 'Maybe,' he said, 'if you use your brain and get stuck into some academic work, you'll have less energy for all this morbid introspection.' So Luther, one day early in the 16th century, was in his study reading Paul's letter to the Romans. He came across that famous phrase: 'The gospel is the power of God to salvation, for in it the righteousness of God is revealed from faith to faith.'

He saw, as in a flash of light, that Paul was there talking about salvation, without sacraments! He was talking about the grace of God being given direct into the hands of faith, without any church ritual intervening. He suddenly saw that he had been on the wrong track all those years. It was a revolutionary insight for him. Suddenly he discovered for the first time the experience of peace of conscience. Though an impeccable Christian, all his striving to earn grace had just made him more and more and more discontented. Now he realized that in salvation grace is given into the empty hands of faith. He did not need sacraments, he did not need to do anything in order to earn it. It was given to him. At last he found peace.

Salvation is not something we attain by religious techniques or earn by good works; it comes to us by grace alone.

That is all very interesting, you may feel, but it is all history. Why should we be talking about legalists in the early church or Catholics in the medieval church? We're neither legalists, nor Catholics. We're Protestants and, after Martin Luther preached this wonderful, Reformation gospel of: 'By grace alone, through faith alone,' this attempt to get round God's charity has at last ended. We're not guilty of any of this. But we are. Let me describe the typical gospel message in a hundred evangelical churches today: 'God laid down the Ten Commandments. Do these, he said, and you'll be OK, you'll go to heaven. But unfortunately we couldn't keep them. So God decided that this was no good; there would be no way of saving anybody if it was just up to the Ten Commandments. He decided he'd have somehow to lower the demands. So he sent Jesus. And as a rsult of what Jesus has done, God can now offer salvation cut-price. Instead of keeping the Ten Commandments, all you have to do is believe.'

## Subtly wrong

As you will notice, something very subtle is wrong with that presentation of the gospel. It is in severe danger of turning faith into a good work. The Catholic turned the sacraments into a good work, without which we could not obtain grace. The legalist turned obedience to the law into a good work, without which grace was no good to us. And some Protestants turn *faith* into a good work, on the merit of which we obtain the grace of Christ. That means we are back to religious technique again; and all down history it has had exactly the same consequences. It means that people do not feel secure in Christ, they lack assurance. Just as Luther lamented that he had never performed enough penances, so I find people who all the time are tormented by the fear that they have not believed enough. They go to evangelistic meeting after evangelistic meeting, making one 'decision' after another because they never feel sure.

The reason why they do not feel sure is that the teaching they have received leads them instinctively to regard faith as a good work, to which they must contribute to make salvation theirs. They are never sure that they have done it right, properly or thoroughly. They are never sure they've done their five per cent. Therefore they fear that one day they may forfeit eternal life. The sad irony is that they are in precisely the same spiritual unrest as Luther was, and for exactly the same reason – that the gospel of grace has been corrupted with the idea that we have to do something to make it ours.

## A matter solely of God's generosity

As we saw, Paul in Ephesians 2:8–10 is saying the very opposite: salvation is totally a matter of God's generosity. Everything in salvation comes from God. I mean everything, including the faith that receives it. Jesus did not just keep the Ten Commandments, die for us and leave us on our own to the business of believing in him. If that were so, faith would be our good work and we would have ground for boasting. But no, he says, 'By grace you have been saved, through faith,' and this whole matter is not from yourselves, it's a gift. It's not a work, it's a gift of God's grace, one hundred per cent charity.

'Irresistible grace' or effectual calling is simply teaching that. God did not leave the work of salvation for us to appropriate for ourselves. He applies it to our souls, so that we cannot pat ourselves on the back in any way whatsoever. Even faith is a gift. It comes to us in the context not of self-congratulation, but of God-glorification. Think of Peter, when he first got an insight into who Jesus was: 'You are the Christ, the Son of the living God.' What did Jesus say to him? 'Well done, Peter. You did well to work that out'? Not at all. 'Blessed are you, Simon . . . for this was not revealed to you by man, but by my Father in heaven' (Mt 16:16–17). Jesus saw that this illumination, this faith of Peter's, was a gift – a gift of

God's grace. So it is always. It is the Lord who opens the heart to respond to the message. And that is what irresistible grace is all about.

## There are problems

All these truths have problems for us, however, because of our limited understanding. In particular, there are three problems that seem to recur constantly and cause people anxiety. These have been touched on already, but need to be faced squarely.

The first is: 'Surely this contradicts free will?' The second is: 'Surely it means people are predestined to hell?' And the third is: 'Surely this discourages evangelism?'

The fascinating thing is that Paul faces all three in his letter to the Romans, chapters 9 and 10. The problems arise for Paul as he considers a fact about which he feels very intensely: the fact that his fellow Jews are not Christians. That makes him upset, indeed broken-hearted. He says, 'I could wish that I myself were cursed and cut off from Christ for the sake of my brothers, those of my own race' (Rom 9:3). He would go to hell, if that would send them to heaven. It is important to realize that for Paul the Jews' unbelief was not merely an emotional problem. It was a theological problem.

At the end of chapter 8, Paul had been showing that we can be sure of going to heaven because our salvation does not depend on ourselves, but on God's eternal purpose and electing grace. God has predestined us. God has this great purpose in which Christians are involved. Therefore we can be sure, whatever happens to us, that nothing can separate us from the love of God. We may have this security, because it does not in any way depend on us. It hinges on God's purpose, his election.

Now the problem is that the Jews rejected the Christian message, when surely they were God's elect too. Yet, despite all their privileges as members of God's elect people, the Jews do not believe. How then can the Christian feel secure in his salvation? If the covenant with Israel proved so unreliable, why should he feel so sure that nothing can separate him from Christ's love? The Jew seems to illustrate the very thing that Paul (at the end of Romans 8) says *cannot* happen – the promise of God failing. Can a people be God's elect and then, by their own decision, reject his blessing? That is the question we all want to ask. Can God elect a person who then rejects his election? Can God fail in his purpose? If he can, there is no assurance in the fact that he has a purpose, because we can thwart it. That is the problem which Paul perceives and feels: an intensely emotional problem and, beyond that, an immensely theological one – the problem of the unbelieving Jews.

## 'God's word has not broken down'

The way Paul answers is as significant as the content of his answer. The first point to notice is the answer he rejects. He will not allow that God's word has broken down. 'It is not as though God's word had failed' (9:6). In saying that, he is rejecting what we may call the 'free will defence'. That is, he does not use the solution which an Arminian or a Pelagian would put to this problem. On their view, God's purpose to save is always conditional on man doing his bit, on man's own inherent power of choice. God cannot save men in spite of themselves, according to the Pelagians and the Arminians. With gentlemanly reserve, he refuses to exert his power in such a way as to contradict man's free will. 'So,' they say, 'election (which Paul is talking about in Romans 8) is not an act of omnipotence.' To them (as chapter 2 showed) it is merely an act of omniscience. God foresees who is going to decide to believe. He does not do anything about it, he simply knows it beforehand. He foresees who is going to be saved by virtue of their own response to the gospel, and he elects them. So run the Arminian and Pelagian views of election. 'The Jews have simply chosen not to believe,' they say; 'There's nothing God can do about that.'

To Pelagians or Arminians three statements are enough to

sort out Paul's problem. The free will defence is: (a) it is the Jews' own fault; (b) they should have believed; (c) they didn't and there's *nothing* God can do about it. You can't blame God. Now that free will defence was available to Paul. He was no idiot; he could think that through. If he had believed that to be the situation, this whole problem would have been solved by the end of verse 6. He feels it necessary to go into this very difficult chapter because he does not believe the free will case.

Paul was neither an Arminian nor a Pelagian. 'It is not as though God's word had failed', it is not as though human choice has thwarted God's purpose. That is not the way it is. That would be an easy and convenient answer, but that it is not true. It would be very nice, very logical, very tidy for us all, if we could see that as the answer to the problem. But the apostle, this man inspired by the Spirit of God who constrains us by his authority today in the word of God, says that that does not fit the facts. It is *not* as though the word of God has failed, or the will of man triumphed.

## God's purpose has triumphed

What then is the answer? It is quite clearly that God's purpose has triumphed, but not in the way that some anticipated. He points out that not all who are descended from Israel are actually Israel. There are in fact two Israels. One is the political nation, to whom the covenant of temporal blessings and the physical land of Canaan were given; the other is the spiritual people, who have inherited the spiritual blessings of forgiveness and eternal life. The covenant was never a blanket arrangement, by which everybody who claimed physical descent from Abraham could share the relationship with God that Abraham knew. Those who knew those blessings were always an elect group within the Jewish nation as a whole.

To prove his point, he cites two examples. Firstly, Isaac and Ishmael, both children of Abraham: one was a participant in the promises, one was not. 'It is not the natural children who are God's children, but it is the children of the promise who are regarded as Abraham's offspring' (9:8).

Secondly, Jacob and Esau, the twin sons of Isaac, of whom only one was elect. 'Rebecca's children had one and the same father, our father Isaac. Yet, before the twins were born or had done anything good or bad – in order that God's purpose in election might stand: not by works but by him who calls – she was told, "The older will serve the younger"' (9:10–12). Paul is pointing out that God makes this declaration before the children were born, so that no one can say that they were elected because of the kind of person they were. 'It is not by works,' he says, 'but by him who calls' (9:12). God made his choice before they were born or had done anything good or bad.

In both cases, God contradicts the natural choice of men, ignoring the existing child and miraculously enabling a barren woman to bear. In human terms, he chooses the less attractive person, and ignores the human rules of primogeniture and inheritance. He does this to assert his own purpose over and against human purposes.

So there are two Israels, he says, the physical and the spiritual. Only the latter is the true elect of God. They have not rejected the Messiah, like the 7,000 who did not bow the knee to Baal in the days of Elijah. There is still a remnant of the Jewish nation who have been saved by God's grace. The purpose of God has not failed, he says. On the contrary, it continues to achieve its goals with infallible certainty.

## Is God unfair?

That is Paul's answer, but it still leaves us with other problems. Uncannily, Paul anticipates them. He is not so stupid as not to know what people will say when he rejects the free will defence and asserts this instead. He raises the objections himself. 'What then shall we say? Is God unjust?' (9:14). 'One of you will say to me: "Then why does God still blame us? For who resists his will?"' (9:19). He is getting at the very subject of irresistible grace. 'God's election is arbitrary, irresistible.'

Therefore, they say, 'God is unfair to act in this way.'

It is when Paul responds to those two arguments that our submission to the authority of Scripture is supremely tested. For his answers are not palatable – and that's an understatement. Many human minds regard Paul's reply to these objections as totally repugnant.

He simply repudiates the charge that God is unfair: 'Is God unjust? Not at all' (9:14). He gives two grounds for denying the charge. The first is the nature of God's grace. It is the essence of mercy to be free. '[God] says to Moses, "I will have mercy on whom I have mercy, and I will have compassion on whom I have compassion"' (9:15). That is putting it positively. When Moses asked for some assurance of God's favour to the chosen people, God replies in effect: 'That's my business. I support whom I choose. It is of the nature of mercy to be free.'

What's more, Paul also puts it negatively, citing the example of Pharaoh. 'For the Scripture says to Pharaoh: "I raised you up for this very purpose, that I might display my power in you and that my name might be proclaimed in all the earth"' (9:17). Once again, it is God's prerogative to be free, whether in bestowing mercy or in withholding it. Verse 18: 'God has mercy on whom he wants to have mercy, and he hardens whom he wants to harden' (9:18). This is not God being arbitrary, this is the essence of mercy. Justice is about what people deserve. If we want to come to God on the basis of justice, then we can go to hell, because that is what we deserve. If we come to God on the basis of mercy, then we have to accept that he has the sovereign right to bestow it or withhold it, as *he* chooses. That is what mercy is. He does not owe it to us. We have no right to it. The first point that needs to be proved by those who want to accuse God of injustice is that we have any claim on God's mercy at all. But we have none. Should God deny us mercy, we would have no valid complaint against God, because he would be just. We are not asking for wages, but for charity.

**'He doesn't deserve to be let off'**

The point is made in a story from Napoleon's day. A soldier had committed some crime, and Napoleon said that he deserved to be shot. His mother came and begged Napoleon: 'Sire, have mercy! Please let him off this terrible punishment.' To which Napoleon replied: 'Why? He doesn't deserve to be let off.' 'Sire,' she responded, 'if he deserved it, it wouldn't be mercy.' That's exactly it – if he deserved it, it wouldn't be mercy. That is Paul's first answer to those who accuse God of injustice.

Paul's second ground for rebuffing the thought that God is unfair concerns man's nature as a creature. 'One of you will say to me: "Then why does God still blame us? For who resists his will?" But who are you, O man, to talk back to God? Shall what is formed say to him who formed it, "Why did you make me like this?"' (9:19–20). Here is another crunch issue. Ultimately it is not so much the arbitrariness of God that offends us as the implied contradiction of our human self-determination. It's nice to know that God has the world under his control, it's comforting to know that history has a purpose. We are happy to see the universe in that way, but there has to be a reservation for human independence, one little sacrosanct sphere of human autonomy, where we insist that self-rule prevails and where even omnipotence may not invade. God cannot contradict our free will – we say that with desperate confidence.

Paul, however, replies quite simply, 'Why not?' To accuse God of injustice in this matter is not only foolhardy, he says, but also impertinent. 'Shall what is formed say, "Why did you make me like this?" Does not the potter have the right to make out of the same lump of clay some pottery for noble purposes and some for common use?' (9:21). We must not misunderstand Paul with this potter and clay analogy. He is not saying that God superimposes some external constraint on human beings and forces them to go against their nature. Martin Luther wrote a great tract *On the Bondage of the Will*.

But when he said in it, 'I deny free will,' he knew that man does have the psychological freedom to act according to his own nature and desires. He was not denying that – only a fool would. It is obvious that we have that freedom. What Luther was saying is that, first of all, the human will is corrupt; and precisely because it is corrupt, our freedom is in fact a curse, for our free will disobeys God. The essence of our rebellion is that we live as if we could choose outside God's will, when we cannot.

The other thing Luther was saying is that God's providence includes everything. If God so wants, he can take away our health, our sanity, our life. Why then do we pretend that there is something inalienable, untouchable, about our power of choice? Every atom in our brains is sustained by God. Every neurone firing away as I think is sustained by God's providence. We cannot take one breath without our Creator's personal permission. How much less can we make a decision independent of him?

## Based on a myth

The idea of free will is based upon the myth that God is excluded from some corner of the universe and that his providence does not extend there. It is not so. The only unconditionally free agent in this universe is God. All the freedom we have lies within the permissive limits of his sovereign purpose. That is not tyranny, that is just deity. It is part of what it means to be God that he 'interferes' with everything and can do nothing else. Our role is to accept that interference, not to begrudge it to him. The truth is that we resent God's deity and are jealous of our free will, because we are not content to be creatures. That is the pride that ruined Adam, the arrogance that still grasps at divine prerogatives ('you will be like God' Gen 3:5) and the insane ambition that still haunts us. Says Paul, we have to learn better, the gospel has got to teach us better, we have to be willing to be creatures.

## Outrageous arrogance

It is therefore not so much that Paul rejects the free will defence, as that he even refuses to contemplate it. He sees it as an act of outrageous arrogance. Man is not on this earth to question God, but to worship him; not to accuse him of injustice, but to bow wonderingly at the complexity of his intelligence. This free will defence is unacceptable precisely because it reduces God. It excludes him from the human heart, saying: 'God, you can't interfere there, because that's my business, that's my private life, that's my territory. You can't interfere there, God.' Paul's answer is simply, 'Why not? You are a creature; you are not a god.'

I said that we would not like it. But we need to keep the balance that Paul sets, because unbelievers can press Paul's argument too far and say: 'Oh well, if I'm predestined to be saved, I shall be. What's the point of bothering?' Or believers can press it too far and say: 'Well, what's the point of evangelizing? If they are going to be saved, they will be.'

It is very important to see that Paul also realized that people are likely to follow that line. So he follows up his very tough emphasis on the sovereignty of God, with a very strong emphasis on the responsibility of man. 'What then shall we say? That the Gentiles, who did not pursue righteousness, have obtained it, a righteousness that is by faith; but Israel, who pursued a law of righteousness, has not attained it. Why not? Because they pursued it not by faith but as it were by works' (9:30–32). We are tempted to think that Paul is going back on all that he has just said. Is he perhaps explaining the Jews' failure to be saved not on the basis of God's purpose any longer, but on the nature of their response? This looks like the free will defence coming in again by the back door, but it is not. Paul here is giving us not the reason for God's election, but the reason for man's condemnation. He is not saying: 'This is the reason God chose you.' He is saying rather: 'This is the reason God condemns you.' Men and women are not sent to hell because they are unlucky enough not to be chosen;

they are sent to hell because they are rebellious sinners who refuse to repent, who refuse to seek God's righteousness through faith.

This is not Paul being crafty with his words; it is an important point. The Bible says that people are saved by grace, but condemned by justice. Election has to do with salvation and is a gracious work that God does not owe us, but which in freedom he elects to give. Condemnation is an act of justice. Hell is where people go by their own fault.

## Responsible for our destiny

We must never so press the doctrine of grace, then, as to obscure the fact that human beings are responsible for their destiny. We may find it difficult to separate those two ideas, but we can see how that difficulty arises. It is rooted in wrongly associating two things: being responsible and being capable. We instinctively assume that if we are responsible for something, then we must be able to do it. If a man is not able to do something, he cannot be held responsible for not doing it, can he? The Bible's doctrine of salvation hinges on the fact that man is responsible to God, but that he does not have the ability to please God and will be justly punished for that failure.

A bankrupt may be totally unable to meet his debts and yet be still accountable for them. And sinners, who are quite unable to stop sinning, will not be able to offer their inability as a defence on the day of judgement. We will not be allowed to say, 'I couldn't help it,' because deep in our hearts we will all know we are responsible for our actions. The weakness of our nature, the deprivations of our upbringing, the perversions of our culture and even God's decision to withhold the Holy Spirit from us – none of these will be an extenuating circumstance that we may plead. They are not valid excuses. Men are condemned because they are responsible for their actions.

As Paul spells out in chapter 10, we are responsible, among

other things, to seek salvation. 'The word is near you.' It's not difficult to get saved, he says. It's not as if you had to go a hundred miles to find out about it or to get hold of it. It's right here. You're responsible to receive it. 'If you confess with your mouth, "Jesus is Lord," and believe in your heart that God raised him from the dead, you will be saved' (Rom 10:9). That is all God requires, he says – the sincerity and commitment of that confession. He will not give assurance to a hypocrite or a coward, but he will give assurance of salvation to anybody who makes that confession; 'He who believes in him will not be disappointed' (10:11). It is important to notice that Paul does not limit this promise to the elect. He insists that it is genuinely extended to every man or woman, irrespective of racial or religious background. 'Everyone who calls on the name of the Lord will be saved' (10:13).

**Responsible to evangelize**

This free gospel of mercy is something we have to offer people, to share with them. We have a responsibility to evangelize. 'How, then, can they call on the one they have not believed in? And how can they believe in the one of whom they have not heard? And how can they hear without someone preaching to them?' (10:14).

Irresistible grace must not be pressed to deny human responsibility. We have to hold these two Bible doctrines in tension, recognizing them both as true. We cannot believe in Christ without a work of grace in our hearts. Once that work of grace is in our hearts, nothing can stop us believing. 'All the Father gives me shall come to me,' says Jesus. There is no doubt about it. Yet we are responsible for our unbelief. We cannot use lack of grace as an excuse for our impenitence. Those two truths have to be preached together. The Scriptures themselves reject the simplistic answer of the free will defence, and say that we must seek an answer within the bounds of that difficult, but creative tension.

All through history men have been trying to obtain God's

grace by way of human technique. 'Ah,' says the ritualist, 'you want God to bless you? You must have the right ceremony, offer the right sacrifices, say the approved liturgy, employ the official priest, make use of the appointed sacraments – that's the technique.'

'Ah,' says the moralist, 'you want to find God's grace? You must heed all God's commandments. You must make your life absolutely holy. You must say your prayers. You must love your neighbour. You must give to charity. That's the way of getting hold of God's grace.'

'Ah,' says the Arminian, 'you want to find God's grace? Believe, make your decision, exert your human free will to receive Christ, commit your life to him – and you will obtain the grace you want.'

In each case, the suggestion is that God responds to man's initiative. Like some mechanical blessing dispenser, God will churn out the spiritual goodies, if man inserts the right religious coin. It's a matter of technique. The ritualist puts his faith in ceremonial, the moralist in loving his neighbour, and the evangelical in 'faith'.

They are all caricatures of what the Bible says. Spiritual blessings do not come to us as a reward; the grace of God is, by definition, an act of unprovoked generosity. God is not responding to us. He is not being manipulated by us. When God gives his grace to a man, it is never because he must, but always because he freely chooses to do so. It's a matter of his election. That is why faith, properly understood, is not a technique for obtaining grace. Faith is not a good work, but a cry of helplessness. It is the confession that I have no good works to offer, nothing to bring. Faith is not a demand on God's justice, but an appeal to God's free mercy. Supremely, faith is not an achievement, but a gift of the Holy Spirit.

That is crucial. Naturally we want to complain about it, to say that it is unfair, that God is being arbitrary. We want to put God in the dock and demand: 'Why?' But we will never get an answer to that question, because our indignation is itself a confession of our human pride and arrogance. We are furious, because our human religious techniques have not worked. God has frustrated them. We call him 'arbitrary' because he does not keep our rules. We call him 'unfair', because he will not play the game our way. We had it all worked out: we did this and this and this for him, and he would do that and that and that for us. It was, we felt, a most satisfactory arrangement.

## God has spoiled our plans

And now God has spoiled our plans, because he has rejected our bargain and refused our contract. In place of them, he offers a completely different route to grace altogether. He tells us that we must trust him, even though his actions are sometimes quite unpredictable (to us) and apparently irrational. He tells us that we must depend on his grace, a grace that seems to be dispensed entirely at his whim, and in complete disregard of any merit. He tells us we have to rely on his mercy, even though we have no right at all to expect to receive it, nor any means at our disposal to guarantee that we shall. No wonder we feel angry! We wanted to keep the reins of our destiny in our own hands, but God will not let us. He will not be our puppet; he insists on being our Sovereign. He will *give* us grace; he will not allow us to claim it.

There have always been two kinds of religion in the world: religions that seek to do God a favour, and religions that seek the favour of God. Religions that think to earn heaven, and those that know man can only beg for it. Religions of works and religions of faith. Religions of techniques and religions of grace. Religions in which men choose God and religions in which God chooses men. What God asks us is: 'What kind of religion is in the New Testament? What kind of religion is yours?'

## Questions on God's grace

Q: If we can't help sinning, how are we responsible for it?

A: None of us will deny that we are responsible for our actions. When we stand before God on the last day, and he judges us for our sins, we will know in our hearts that we made sinful choices and that we are responsible for those choices. Yet we are also, as a matter of human experience, in bondage to sin. Not one of us is sinless, or could be sinless, by our own natural ability. By nature we are sinners; we know that we are going to remain sinners and that we're caught in a web of sin, from which we cannot extricate ourselves.

We have referred to Pharaoh before, because he is one of the most telling examples. In Exodus the hardening of Pharaoh's heart is expressed in three different ways. (1) 'Pharaoh's heart became hard and he would not listen to them' (Ex 7:13). That is a state of nature; his heart was hard – that's just how he was. (2) 'When Pharaoh saw that there was relief, he hardened his heart and would not listen to Moses' (Ex 8:15). That was a voluntary decision on Pharaoh's part. He was responsible for the hardening of his heart there. (3) 'The Lord hardened Pharaoh's heart, and he would not let the Israelites go' (Ex 11:10). To the state of nature and a voluntary choice has been added God's judicial decree. God was confirming Pharaoh in that state.

If people go to hell, it is because God confirms them in their decision and in that natural state in which they already are. He gives them what they have already said they want. They want independence of him; he gives it to them. They want to turn their back on him, they do not want him in their universe – all right, they will not have God in their universe. He gives them what they want. Reprobation is not a decree of God in the same way that election is, because in order to save us, God has to reverse the situation completely. But hell is where we are going, where we want to go. All that God has to do to send us there is to say: 'You will have what you want.' But to save us, he has to do what he did for the Jews – work a miracle to bring them out of Egypt. And that requires a great saving act of his initiative.

Q: How free are our wills?

A: This question crops up under the heading of 'total depravity', but it also occurs under the theme of grace and it is worth setting out the two problems about free will. One is the fact that we are sinners: our wills are in bondage to sin and, when we choose, we always choose wrong. We are a little like people standing on a slope; it's always easier to go down than up. Adam was standing on the level. He was not corrupt, so his will was not inclined to evil in the way ours now is by nature. In that sense, he had a 'free' will, but his will became limited as ours is by the Fall. The second problem with free will is that we are creatures and cannot operate outside the sovereign providence of God. The ultimate fact that limits the freedom of the will is that we cannot choose outside the bounds of God's permission, because we are creatures – any more than anything else in this universe can happen outside the bounds of his permission. No one, Adam included, has or had free will of that second order. God alone has free will ultimately – which is why he can bestow grace.

Q: How does God's sovereignty relate to Romans 10:9: 'If you confess with your mouth, "Jesus is Lord," and believe in your heart . . . you will be saved'?

A: Believing in your heart is not earning you salvation. It is the confession of faith, which evidences regeneration in the heart. There is no way that a person can make that confession and say, 'Jesus is Lord,' but by the Holy Spirit. Paul is here giving assurance of salvation: if a person sincerely and publicly makes that confession, that shows that there has been a work of grace in that person's life. They could not otherwise make that confession sincerely and publicly. By saying, 'Jesus is Lord,' you are just stating a fact about what your heart now sees to be true.

Q: What if the Ethiopian eunuch had not stopped his chariot to be baptized? What if the woman with the issue of blood had not touched the hem of Christ's garment? What if Naaman had refused to dip himself in the Jordan? Would they have been saved?

A: God does require obedience from us and the benefits of salvation flow to us as we are obedient; there is no doubt about that. But, having performed those acts of obedience and of faith, did those who performed them feel that they had reason to congratulate themselves? Did the Ethiopian congratulate himself on his judgement? Or the woman go home patting herself on the back? No, she went home saying, '*Jesus* is wonderful.' God was working all along, not just in the moment when those people (and any others) 'came to faith' in conscious experience. It was not a question of either/or – either *God* stopped the chariot or the Ethiopian did; when God works, you cannot separate the two, for God is over all.

Q: What about people who have never heard the gospel (e.g. Romans 2:12–16)?

A: I do not think the Bible ever fully answers the question of the people who have never heard. There are one or two hints and this verse in Romans is the biggest. The Bible never says much about this question for this simple reason: anyone who has a Bible in their hands does not belong to that category. The Bible is not given to satisfy our curiosity and has no interest in answering all the questions that you and I might like to put. It is clear that God's judgement cannot, for those people who have never heard the gospel, be on the same basis as for those who have – though it will still be a judgement.

Q: Has it not been a great spur to missionary zeal that people have believed that there can be no salvation unless the gospel is preached?

A: Yes. Scholars have argued that if God so chooses, he can work through his Spirit without his word. It would be over-dogmatic to say that someone who has never heard cannot be saved, though we do not have any evidence that such have been. But, if they *are* saved, it must be by active electing grace through the Spirit alone in their lives, without a conscious response to a preached word. If God wants to save someone without his word, on what basis may we say that he cannot? But it is certainly true that the normal means of grace is the word, and Romans 10:14 must be our spur: 'How can they hear without a preacher?' It would be very dangerous to allow speculations (about 'what if?' and 'couldn't God?') to deter us from obedience to the way he says we must go about it.

Q: 'Grace' seems arbitrary. How can we present it to the non-Christian?

A: If a person is humble, there is great encouragement in grace for the seeking unbeliever. What do you say to the person who says: 'I'd love to be a Christian because I can see you Christians have got a lot, but I just can't believe'? If you do not believe in all-powerful grace, you can only say: 'Hard cheese. It's up to you. Try harder.' That does not help. But if you believe in grace, you can say something to them and do something for them. You can tell them to pray; you too can pray. You cannot pray, if God cannot interfere with a person's 'free will'. But we can pray for our unconverted friend, because grace is a gift; we can ask God, in his mercy, to give it to them. They can claim God's promise: 'Ask and it will be given to you; seek and you will find; knock and the door will be opened to you' (Mt 7:7). They can ask God for faith. They can say: 'God, I don't even know if you exist. But something in my heart is calling me into this Christianity. If you're there, please make yourself real to me. Please give me this faith these Christians talk about.' God never denies that prayer. The mere fact that they have got to that point of seeking is evidence of a work of grace in their lives. I feel terrifically encouraged when someone says to me: 'I'd like to be a Christian, but I can't.' I know they would not want to be a Christian unless God were already down the road with them quite a few miles. Grace is not arbitrary; it is encouraging. It gives us something positive to offer.

Q: How does this view of grace relate to mass evangelism?

A: It puts some qualification on mass evangelism, but it would be wrong to exaggerate it. Nothing takes away from that hymn: 'O happy day that fixed *my* choice.' It's a conscious, personal choice – our wills are involved; but the ability and motivation to make that choice derives solely from God's grace. People have to make decisions to become Christians. And the preacher has to call on people in the imperative: 'Repent! Believe!' We issue a command. Do you know that picture in Ezekiel of the valley of dry bones? God says to Ezekiel: 'Now preach at them!' What a stupid thing to do! That is exactly what a preacher is doing, when unbelievers are present: he is preaching to dead bones. A very stupid thing to do? No. He is preaching in belief that God the Spirit is going to accompany the word and bring new life. So 'get up out of your seats' is not too far from what Ezekiel told them to do.

But when a decisionist approach to evangelism is pressed too far, it may communicate to the unbeliever that *he* can contribute something to his salvation. Instead of seeing himself as someone just holding out empty hands to God, he may be very subtly encouraged to see himself as doing something for God: 'I did my bit for God to-night. I went forward.' If people go forward in that attitude of mind, (a) they may not be saved at all, or (b) they may be absorbing bad teaching in the way that they are being evangelized – teaching that can leave awful problems of assurance in the weeks that follow.

# *You'll Get There in the End*

*by*

Greg Haslam

The fact and the implication of God's grace are tremendously liberating, but we all finally want to know whether grace has guaranteed our future. We sing hymns that ring again and again with affirmations of the perseverance of the saints. It makes a mockery of those words, however, if remnants of doubt linger in our minds about whether we will get to heaven. If we are not sure that we will, we are mouthing meaningless words as we sing.

The question therefore is this: now that I am a Christian, will I remain one for the rest of my life? The converted slave-trader, John Newton, was in absolutely no doubt that he would. His famous hymn 'Amazing Grace' closes with these words:

> Through many dangers, toils and snares
> I have already come.
> 'Twas grace that brought me safe thus far,
> And grace will lead me home.

That strikes a vital note of realism. When we think of the perseverance of the saints, we are not looking at the future through rose-tinted glasses, as if it will be free from trials and difficulties. What God does assert is that his grace is sufficient to see us through every last one of them. Another great Christian, John Charles Ryle (the first bishop of Liverpool last century), was in no doubt that he would get there in the end. He said that

> There are two points on which the teaching of the Bible is very plain and distinct: one is the fearful danger of the ungodly, the other the perfect safety of the righteous.

A 20th-century writer, G. I. Williamson, puts the basic question and gives the biblical answer:

> When a person has been regenerated or born again by the Holy Spirit and truly converted to Christ through repentance and faith, is it possible to again become a child of wrath and of eternal destruction? The answer of the Scripture is clear and emphatic: no, it is not possible.

## The only result

This seems almost too good to be true. It looks as though we are taking all the positives and overlooking all the negatives – as though we are exaggerating the Bible's promises to us as Christians and ignoring its warning and cautions. We will look at those later, but the 'perfect safety' of the believer is only the result of all the truths we have already seen in earlier chapters.

If I believed, like a Roman Catholic or an Arminian, that in some way God's will is not completely sovereign, but that man's will can intervene or abort his purposes, then I would be entirely consistent to doubt my security. We have no reason to doubt the keeping power of God, but if we allow our security to depend in any way on our fickle wills, then we sense that we could very easily unsave ourselves. If we could decide against the purposes of God, we know that our future is very uncertain indeed.

God, however, remains invincible in his purposes. God is God. By his all-conquering resurrection power he drew us to himself. No power, outside us or inside us, is greater than that. Jesus said: 'No-one can come to me unless the Father who sent me draws him, and I will raise him up at the last day'

(Jn 6:44). The one he draws on the first day of Christian experience he will raise on the last day. The Christian will stick at it to the end. That may astonish us, knowing ourselves as we do. It astonishes me, knowing myself as I do. But it is what the Bible emphatically teaches, You will never die, never perish. God will never cast you aside, never disinherit you from his family, never reject you. You are destined to spend eternity with Jesus Christ. That is the perseverance of the saints.

## No matter what?

We need to be clear as to what that perseverance does *not* mean. It does not mean that every person who goes forward at the end of an evangelistic meeting, or makes some decision while sitting in their seat, or signs a card in a counselling room will be saved at the last. It does not mean that everyone who claims to be a Christian and says, 'Yes, I'm a believer,' will be saved, no matter what happens. It does not mean that everyone who has been christened as an infant, or baptized by immersion on profession of faith, or joined the membership of a church will eventually be in heaven. It does not mean, by contrast, that only the super-saints will get there – the heroes and martyrs, the outstanding godly people in all those biographies.

It means positively that true believers – simple, ordinary Christians, known and unknown – will get to heaven, all of them. We can feel fairly sure about elderly Christians, those who are teetering on the edge of eternity and have just a few weeks or days left. It is reasonably certain that they will stay in the faith.

I knew a man who came to the Lord and then was taken into eternity less than a fortnight later. It is not hard to be certain that he died secure, but then we think: 'Well, I'd be pretty assured about my own future if I were to die in the next fortnight. But I may have fifty years ahead of me. How can I possibly predict how it will be with me then?'

## Now and then

The Bible shows that you can know now how it will be then. The perseverance of the saints does not relate merely to the aged or those about to die. This does not mean that temptation will never come your way, that you will never encounter difficulties, never lapse, never grow cold, never prove unfaithful in this area or that. This truth does not mean that you will be free from terrible assaults of the devil on your faith, or from gross doubts and fears. The Bible is replete with examples of believers who endured tremendous difficulties and fell in the face of fierce temptations – Noah got drunk; Abraham lied out of fear for his own and his wife's safety; Jonah ran away from the clear and declared will of God; David, the great king and anointed one of Israel, committed adultery; and Peter, in an act of supreme cowardice, denied the Lord before a servant girl. The examples are numerous.

We will not necessarily be preserved from such gross lapses into sin. Grace is available to make a way of escape from temptation, but that is not the point of this doctrine. John Murray has said:

> It is true that the believer does sin. He may fall into grievous sins and backslide for lengthy periods. But it is also true that a believer cannot abandon himself to sin. He cannot come once more under the dominion of sin. He cannot be guilty of certain kinds of unfaithfulness.

Perseverance does not mean a life free from the pain of failure or the pressure of temptation.

Those are some negatives; now to the positives. This is how it will affect our experience as believers in Christ: God will ensure without a shadow of doubt that we will never fall absolutely headlong, never fall completely and finally away from him. If we trip up or seriously lapse in our Christian living, we will sooner or later rise again from those lapses to a fresh walk with God, to a renewed commitment to Jesus Christ, and to the true discipleship from which we temporarily departed. We can never be lost: the saints – those called by God, to whom faith is given by grace – will persevere to the end. Two parties are involved in this: God and ourselves. The supreme and conclusive reason why we can never be lost is that God has guaranteed to preserve us. It does not rest on us in the first – or final – instance.

## God continuously at work

What the Bible says about our responsibility to continue always assumes that God is continuously doing the greater work for us. God will preserve us; that is why we will make it in the faith. The first focus is on God's work – he preserves; and he works so that our responsibilities may come to the fore – we persevere. These assertions are all consistent with the other great truths in this book. That is fine, but the important question is not whether they are logically consistent with each other, but whether the Bible teaches them. So we turn directly to its pages.

The Scriptures demonstrate that God's work runs concurrently with ours. They do not give any credit to us, but show that the grace of God elicits some activity from us and in us, as he preserves and keeps us. Put at its simplest, he preserves and we persevere. We persevere because he preserves. Many passages hold these twin truths together. 'Keep yourselves in God's love,' states our duty to persevere. 'To him who is able to keep you from falling and to present you before his glorious presence without fault' (Jude 24), states his power to preserve. Revelation 3:10 makes the same two points: 'Since you have kept my command to endure patiently, I will also keep you from the hour of trial that is going to come upon the whole world.' Philippians 2:12 exhorts us to keep going: 'Continue to *work out* your own salvation with fear and trembling' (italics mine) and then it adds the reason, 'For it is God who *works in* you to will and to act according to his good purpose.'

The Bible's evidence of this double-sided truth is absolutely overwhelming, but it does not present it as a fifty/fifty proposition – as though we do half and God does half. God does it all; when we get to glory it will be one hundred per cent due to God. We persevere only because he preserves us, but that is why it is also one hundred per cent us. The decisions we make, the resistance we offer to temptation, the way we walk with God – our perseverance rests one hundred per cent on those, as they rest one hundred per cent on him. So we need to be persuaded of the preserving power of God.

This is clear as daylight in Philippians 1:6. As Paul writes from a prison cell to encourage Christians and to sort out their difficulties, he strikes this positive note: 'Being confident of this, that he who began a good work in you will carry it on to completion until the day of Jesus Christ.' Paul would not allow his readers (then or now) to add any 'Yes, but' at the end of that sentence. The same concept is repeated: 'He will keep you strong to the end, so that you will be blameless on the day of our Lord Jesus Christ' (1 Cor 1:8). He *will* keep you strong.

## Rescued from every attack

This is reinforced: 'The Lord will rescue me from every evil attack' (2 Tim 4:18). In Paul's experience, 'every evil attack' included the hostility of men. He knew, however, that there were subtler, stronger attacks as well. He was writing from his final dungeon cell in Rome, waiting to be beheaded by the Roman authorities. He knew that 'our struggle is not against flesh and blood, but against . . . the powers of this dark world and against the spiritual forces of evil in the heavenly realms' (Eph 6:12). He had in mind the final onslaughts on his soul which would surely take place as he awaited martyrdom. He knew the devil's sharp desire to make this great apostle tremble at the very last and denounce the faith at the Roman executioner's block. But his assurance was this: 'The Lord will rescue me from every evil attack, and will bring me safely to his heavenly kingdom.'

His assurance echoes in his prayer for the Thessalonian

believers:

> May your whole spirit, soul and body be kept blameless at the coming of our Lord Jesus Christ. The one who calls you is faithful and he will do it (1 Thess 5:23–24).

Hebrews 13:5 says the same: 'God has said, "Never will I leave you; never will I forsake you."' Particularly fascinating is Romans 8:29-30, because it takes us through the themes of this book:

> For those God foreknew he also predestined to be conformed to the likeness of his Son, that he might be the firstborn among many brothers. And those he predestined, he also called; those he called, he also justified; those he justified, he also glorified.

We have seen that this is called 'the golden chain of salvation', with five links: God foreknows us; God predestines us; God calls us; God justifies us; and God glorifies us. Astonishingly, these verses take us from eternity past to eternity future, through five profound words. Each of those words focuses on God's elected, redeemed people, the uncountable multitude for whom Christ died. In eternity past God foreknew and predestined us. Then he began to work out his purposes in time in our own experience. He gave his effective call that brought us to faith in Christ. At the same moment he justified us.

What is left after that? Our whole lifetime, of course. But Paul does not mention that, and we want to say to him: 'Hold on, Paul. I do know forgiveness, I do hear what you say about being justified. But what about my whole life ahead of me? What about all its ups and downs, its temptations and trials?' Paul's thought leaps right over this life to assure us that our glorification is already achieved and settled. It is not that Paul ignores this life and its human uncertainties; it is just that the one crucial factor is what God has done, is doing and will do. That is why he jumps from justification to glorification, for the glory will simply be our sanctification completed. What God starts he rounds off. Those chosen in eternity past are taken through time to glory, with no exceptions, no failures, no drop-outs.

That is the golden chain of salvation. Everyone who believes has been justified. Every justified person has been called. Everyone called was predestined. Everyone predestined to glory will get there. None can fall short. The basis for this exhilarating fact is Romans 8:28: 'We know that in all things God works for the good of those who love him, who have been called according to his purpose.' In *all* things: in everything that enters your mind, or happens to you, or comes into your experience, or puts pressure on you. In all things God is working for the good of those who love him. If God is working for us, who can be against us? (8:31.)

## Another guarantee

All this is bound up with another guarantee which God has made to us. We are safe because God has pledged himself to the legal covenants and promises that he has made to us. God has sworn a legally binding covenant towards us and confirmed the same with oaths. This comes out in Jesus's teaching. He always spoke the truth, but he prefaced certain statements with a solemn and binding phrase: 'Verily, I say unto you,' or (as the NIV puts it), 'I tell you the truth.' He wanted to draw our attention to what he said, but he also wanted solemnly to affirm that he bound himself to what he said. In John 5 Jesus says three times, 'I tell you the truth' (5:19, 24, 25). In effect he is saying: 'This is worthy of the weight of your whole trust. I am going on record as telling you the truth.' He goes on: 'Whoever hears my word and believes him who sent me has eternal life and will not be condemned; he has crossed over from death to life' (5:24). These are guarantees that the Son of God has made to us; he cannot go back on his word.

Hebrews 6 is a difficult passage, talking about 'if people fall away'. We will return to that chapter, but it is significant that the writer says: 'Even though we speak like this . . . we are confident of better things in your case – things that accompany salvation' (Heb 6:9). How can he be confident, in view of potential falling away? Because of 'what has been promised' by God (6:12) and because 'he confirmed it with an oath' (6:17).

> Men swear by someone greater than themselves, and the oath confirms what is said and puts an end to all argument. Because God wanted to make the unchanging nature of his purpose very clear to the heirs of what was promised, he confirmed it with an oath. [The oath was 'I will surely bless you and give you many descendants.'] God did this so that, by two unchangeable things in which it is impossible for God to lie, we who have fled to take hold of the hope offered to us may be greatly encouraged (6: 16–18).

It is not simply that God has told us: 'I will surely bless you' – though that secures all the future God has for all his people, the sons and daughters of Abraham by faith. It is not merely that a God who cannot lie has said this to us – though it would be enough if he only said it once. God has done more. So that our sceptical, unbelieving, doubting, introspective minds may be assured, God said it once and then confirmed it with an oath. By two unchangeable things, his word and his oath – in which it is impossible for God to lie – we who have fled for refuge may be greatly encouraged. That is an understatement; 'greatly encouraged' means 'absolutely assured'. God said it on oath.

## On oath

Now people can bend laws, wriggle out of sworn statements, twist the rule book and generally find ways round undertakings they do not want to keep. Not so with God. When God gives his word and oath, he will not go back on it and no human or demon can change his mind or get him to bend. So Romans 8:31-34 begins with this challenge: 'What, then, shall we say in response to this? If God is for us, who can be against us?' If God is for us – that is the all-important thing. Only those called and justified can say 'Yes, God is for me.'

There is Paul imagining us in the law courts. He is throwing out a challenge on behalf of all God's people, all the elect, every believer, you and me. He is challenging all the forces in all creation – death and life, angels or demons, present or future, height or depth. 'Who,' he demands, 'will bring any charge against those whom God has chosen?' In other words, who can bring evidence to persuade God to reject us? We say: 'Well, I could bring charges myself . . . my conscience . . . my past . . . .' It does not matter at that point what our conscience says, what our family could tell about us, what our employer knows about us. Most of all, it does not matter what accusations Satan can hurl against us. If God is for us, who can be against us? If God has declared us not guilty, no charges can ever be brought against us, because Jesus has already answered them for us.

## Paul draws his conclusions

Paul draws certain deductions from this: nothing can separate us from the love of Christ, because that love has been legally pledged to us. No upset can surprise God. We often feel that we may fall, because we cannot predict what temptations the devil will throw at us or for how long. But God cannot be taken by surprise about our future. God knows the whole sweep of our earthly existence and will never allow the prosecution to succeed against us.

'God's gifts and his call are irrevocable' (Rom 11:29). That statement is about God's unchanging purposes towards the Jews, but it is a general truth also. It applies to us. God does not give with one hand and take back with the other. He does not bestow now and reclaim later. Someone has called this the 'syllogism of security'. The ancient Greeks argued by syllogisms: each would have a major premiss, a minor premiss, and a conclusion. For example: 'All men are mortal. Socrates is a man. Therefore Socrates is mortal.' Here it is as though Paul is saying: '*Major premiss:* God's gifts and his call cannot be revoked. *Minor premiss:* salvation is the gift and call of God.

*Conclusion:* therefore salvation cannot be recalled.'

A further ground for our security is in the imperishable nature of the eternal life God has granted to us. John 11:25-26 reads: 'I am the resurrection and the life. He who believes in me will live, even though he dies; and whoever lives and believes in me will never die.' Do we believe this? We possess, as believers, nothing less than the life of Christ indwelling us – our body, mind, heart, soul, spirit. God imparted this life to us, as the letter to the Romans teaches, because of the union we have with Christ.

That union means intimate involvement in everything Christ has done. All Christ's saving acts are passed on to our benefit because of our union with Christ. For this reason it is impossible to have died with Christ when he died, to have been buried with him in a tomb, to have been raised along with Christ, and yet to fall short of being more than a conqueror through him who loved us. If Christians can finally fall away before they get to heaven, then all Christ's saving work can be frustrated by you or me, by some lapse on our part. I, for one, find that impossible to believe. It is declared in 1 Peter 1:23, 'You have been born again, not of perishable seed, but of imperishable, through the living and enduring word of God.' Indestructible life is ours.

## The sealing of the Spirit

The sealing of the Spirit confirms this assurance. Whatever our views about when that sealing takes place, it certainly has to do with our conscious knowledge that we have eternal life. Paul writes in Ephesians 1:13:

> You also were included in Christ when you heard the word of truth, the gospel of your salvation. Having believed, you were marked in him with a seal, the promised Holy Spirit.

This includes the assuring witness of the Holy Spirit to our hearts that we are the children of God. We are sealed also in the sense that our salvation cannot be tampered with; we are sealed for delivery to glory.

If it is possible for the believer to fall away, it makes a mockery of the seal of the Holy Spirit. A seal means ownership, security, assurance. The seal of the Holy Spirit is God's witness to us that we are his saved children. But the Holy Spirit is lying, if it is possible for a believer to fall away; he says one thing, but things are not what they seem.

It is sometimes like that with street sellers. You can go shopping in a big city, particularly before Christmas, and as you walk down the street, you may see many unlicensed salesmen offering goods marked with famous brand names. The name on the perfume and the packaging look just right. You soon discover that they are a cheap imitation; the aroma does not last long, even though the perfume is in a 'Chanel No. 19' box and bottle. The Holy Spirit plans no such confidence trick on the believer, labelling us as secure in Christ, yet knowing that the life within us may fade as that perfume did. If the Spirit has sealed us and been given to us as a guarantee of promised glory, the Spirit is no liar. The Spirit's sealing in our hearts is evidence enough that God is going to keep us.

All this positive affirmation of God's power and promises goes hand in hand with God's expectation that we persevere in the faith. John Calvin, the great 16th-century Reformer, spoke of the 'perseverance of *the faith* of God's elect'. The balance between the preserving power of God and the concurrent persevering in faith on our part is in 1 Peter 1:3-5:

> He has given us new birth into a living hope . . . and into an inheritance that can never perish, spoil or fade – kept in heaven for you, who through faith are shielded by God's power until the coming of the salvation that is ready to be revealed in the last time.

Those verses make three points relevant to our theme. First, that we are kept; we have seen the evidence for that. Secondly, that we are kept through faith. Thirdly, that this keeping and believing are *until* the final revealing of our salvation. God will keep us until Christ returns or calls us home; and it is through faith that we are being kept until that same event. Our faith will endure until the end. We are not kept by God, irrespective of whether we do or do not believe. On the contrary, the keeping power of God is there to ensure that we keep on believing.

## Christ interceding

This is enforced by another passage, which illuminates that most consoling truth – the intercession of Christ. It tells us what Jesus Christ is doing, now that he has risen from the dead and ascended to heaven. He still has involvement in our lives and concern for our temptations here on earth. Anything else would be unthinkable for the One who loved his own to the end. The writer to the Hebrews is at pains to demonstrate that Jesus Christ in heaven is doing a great deal for us, even now in our current lives on earth. In particular: 'He is able to save completely [i.e. right to the very end] those who come to God through him, because he always lives to intercede for them' (Heb 7:25).

At this very moment Jesus Christ has your name on his lips as he presents your concerns and your welfare to the Father, as he intercedes for you. If we want to know the thrust of his intercession, the only hint Scripture gives is the kind of praying he did for his disciples while still on earth.

Before his arrest and betrayal, for example, he turned to Simon Peter and said: 'I have prayed for you, Simon, that your faith may not fail' (Lk 22:32). The timing of that prayer tells us something vital. Within hours Simon Peter had lapsed badly, had fallen into a terrible state of cowardice and denunciation of Christ, even with swearing. Had Christ's praying failed? (If it did for Peter, it might for us.) The Saviour's interceding could not go unanswered. This helps us to understand that our security rests ultimately not on our avoiding a fall, but on the intercession of Christ.

To take another example, our Lord prayed as our high priest, as John 17 records. There he makes many requests for all God's people through all time:

> Protect them by the power of your name . . . Protect them from the evil one . . . I want those you have given me to be with me where I am, and to see my glory (Jn 17:11, 15, 24).

Jesus has prayed then and is praying now that we may be with him where he is, and see his glory, that we may get to heaven. It is unthinkable that a Saviour, who lives always to intercede for us, could have his prayers unheeded and see us finally in hell. Impossible. The intercession of Jesus shows that our security is not in the absence of danger, but in the presence of God through those dangers, guaranteeing that we are maintained in the faith.

Robert Murray McCheyne expressed the confidence this brings: 'If I could hear Christ praying for me in the next room, I would not fear a million of enemies. Yet the distance makes no difference; he *is* praying for me!'

To say that a believer could stop believing because of some extreme pressure or danger is to deny not only the power of Christ's intercession, but the very nature of the gospel.

> In the gospel a righteousness from God is revealed, a righteousness that is by faith from first to last [from faith to faith], just as it is written: 'The righteous will live by faith' (Rom 1:17).

Paul there is setting the keynote for the gospel he is going to present in his first eight chapters. At the outset he puts in a nutshell what he understands to be the essence of Christianity: something (a righteousness from God) that is by faith and is from first to last.

The quotation he uses, 'The righteous will live by faith,' comes from the Old Testament prophet, Habakkuk (2:4). That was written against the backdrop of Babylon's impending invasion of Israel. The prophet wonders how a holy God could use such an unholy instrument to chasten his disobedient people? He is absolutely rocked by God telling him that Babylon (the Chaldeans) – that murderous, cruel Third Reich of the ancient world – is going to invade the holy land of Israel to plunder, ruin and take captive. But God tells him it is so, and gives this word: 'The righteous will live by faith.'

God is saying that, despite all the tribulation that will come, the righteous will endure. A sifting and chastening work will go on. But the righteous will stick at it, they will endure through it all. How? By faith. If the righteous are to endure, their faith must keep being exercised. That's why Paul quotes this, because the gospel is a donation of righteousness to a responding faith in our hearts – a faith that God guarantees from first to last.

## Incredible – a rich reward

Knowing our weakness, it is incredible to think that our faith will last, but it will. That Habakkuk reference occurs also in Hebrews 10:35 and its use there clinches the fact that our faith will endure:

> So do not throw away your confidence; it will be richly rewarded. You need to persevere so that when you have done the will of God, you will receive what he has promised. For in just a very little while, 'He who is coming will come and will not delay. But my righteous one will live by faith. And if he shrinks back, I will not be pleased with him.' But we are not of those who shrink back and are destroyed, but of those who believe and are saved.

Sinclair Ferguson has said: 'There is no such thing in Scripture as perseverance without faith . . . but those who have faith will persevere.'

All this seems almost too good to be true. So we must now try to relate it to the various objections that are brought, from Scripture and experience. Which of us has not been horrified to see an apparently keen Christian, perhaps even a leader or prominent figure in the church, initially drifting, then falling and finally even denouncing the faith and denying Christ. We cannot credit this; how can it happen? We must turn to some of the difficult passages of Scripture, aware of the background from which we come. Our 20th-century Christianity has been shallow, with a great deal of easy believism, which has seen a high proportion of professing Christians falling away. Our day therefore has a distaste for strong, assertive statements about our security; and it has a very man-centred view of the Christian life that says: 'It's all up to me.'

The passages we must look at are best seen as safeguards against any distortion of the truths of God's grace. They show what those truths do not mean, as we saw earlier. They warn us against glibly presuming on grace. They alert us to the possibility that people can delude themselves about their salvation. They remind us that God's sovereignty does not eliminate our human responsibility. They are rather like what Paul said about the storm-tossed sailors in the impending shipwreck: 'Unless these men stay with the ship, you cannot be saved' (Acts 27:31). They were saved by means of staying in the ship. Many sobering passages are to ensure that we stick to the means of us getting to heaven (our enduring in the faith, 'staying with the ship'). We get to the shore as we respond seriously and obediently to those warnings. They do not imply that Christians can fall away; they are preservatives, to keep us from falling away.

## The backslider

What then of a passage like Hebrews 6? There are in general in the New Testament three types of trouble into which professing believers can fall. Most of the warning texts deal with one of these three categories. The first is the backslider. Galatians 6:1 describes him as a saint who has been overtaken in some trespass, and exhorts fellow Christians: 'Brothers, if someone is caught in a sin, you who are spiritual should restore him gently.'

Every believer has at some point in his Christian life backslidden, though there are degrees of backsliding. The backslider's fellow Christians have brotherly responsibilities of exhortation and admonition, and then sometimes of church discipline. That may mean telling the church and even, in extreme circumstances, having him put out of the church, with a view to his restoration. The Bible has many examples of backsliders, but they are always eventually restored, as was Jonah.

Dr Martyn Lloyd-Jones had a moving story of a man who had backslidden for twenty years. He had fallen into adultery and abandoned his wife and children. He walked into Westminster Chapel on the very evening when he was contemplating suicide, just at the moment the Doctor was praying: 'Lord, restore the backslider.' He was restored and gloriously brought back to faith in Christ.

## The reject

The second is the reject or castaway. 1 Corinthians 9:27 is a very alarming text which reads: 'I beat my body and make it my slave so that after I have preached to others, I myself will not be disqualified for the prize.' I think I can show that Paul is not talking about losing his salvation at all. That is far from his mind. He has rather been speaking of his ministry as an apostle of Christ. He is saying that it is frighteningly possible for a Christian in service for the Lord, through moral lapse or doctrinal deviation or unwise entanglement with others, to be disqualified from his ministry.

It is possible for him, as it were, to be put on the shelf, to be taken out of that work for the Lord, perhaps never to re-enter it. For example, if the minister of a church fell into adultery, or some kind of sexual promiscuity, and it was discovered, he would have to be put out of the ministry, and it would be extremely unlikely that God would permit him to re-enter it. Paul was afraid that he would be disqualified from his ministry – a reject. He was not thinking about losing his salvation, but about proving derelict in his duty and therefore forfeiting his privileges as a minister of Christ. So he disciplined himself – he pummelled his body.

## The apostate

After the backslider and the castaway, the third category is the apostate. Certain passages describe him: Hebrews 6:4–8; Hebrews 10:26-31 and 2 Peter 2:20-22.

> It is impossible for those who have once been enlightened, who have tasted the heavenly gift, who have shared in the Holy Spirit, who have tasted the goodness of the word of God and the powers of the coming age, if they fall away, to be brought back to repentance, because to their loss they are crucifying the Son of God all over again and subjecting him to public disgrace (Heb 6:4-8).

These passages warn us of a falling away from spiritual influences that entails no possibility of restoration. That is very important. The passage is emphatic: there is no possibility of restoring *these* people. That is why they cause such trouble. I do not believe that these passages are hypothetical. They are not dealing with a man of straw, as if this could never actually occur, as though the writer were just putting something up to frighten us. The language is too strong and too terrifying to be merely painted fire. It is a very real danger. The passages are describing more than an occasional lapse, even into very serious sin. They picture more than Abraham's lying, or David's adultery, or Peter's cowardice under pressure. All of those were restored; all of these it is possible to restore. What the writer is describing is given by the verb he uses in Hebrews 6:4 – a participle from a verb *piptein*. The verb means to fall headlong, to fall absolutely, to fall without remedy and beyond all recovery. A Christian cannot do that.

The sin described is delineated very clearly in Hebrews 10:29:

> How much more severely do you think a man deserves to be punished who has trampled the Son of God under foot, who has treated as an unholy thing the blood of the covenant that sanctified him, and who has insulted the Spirit of grace?

The sin there is a knowing, wilful, diliberate, calculated,

complete rejection of Jesus Christ. It is a wilful turning aside from that which you have been convinced is true. It is to rid yourself entirely of the whole of Christianity, in full awareness of what you are doing. It is a hard-faced impenitence in the light of all the warnings of God and the exhortations of others. It is to remain faithless to the day of your death and so prove finally damned.

Can a Christian possibly do that? The answer is emphatically: 'No, he cannot.' Many of the people whom the writer to the Hebrews addressed were just Jews, who were convinced that Christianity was true, but had not entered into the good of it. That is why Hebrews 3:7–47 is a long exhortation to them to enter into God's rest. 'You're convinced Jesus is who he says he is? Well, enter into God's rest,' he says to them in effect. This ought to alert us that it is possible to be very near to full faith in Christ, but finally to fall short of it. Certainly the description in Hebrews 6:4–6 looks as though it cannot be of anybody else but a Christian!

## Five features

But what do the five points mean, which are true of these people who possibly fall away? They were *once enlightened.* Now, as someone has said, all who have been regenerated have been enlightened, but not all those who have been enlightened have been regenerated. 'Once enlightened' means to be intellectually lit up with the gospel, to perceive it in some way, to come to some grasp and understanding of it and to be convinced that it is true. We have all come across people who can say: 'Yes, I can see that.' They do not have overwhelming intellectual barriers to faith, so we ask: 'Why won't you believe?' But they will not. So near, but so far – enlightened. More than this, they have *tasted the heavenly gift*. Tasted – yes; swallowed – no. They have sensed the power of God's truth and even felt the presence of Jesus. But, as Jesus said to the crowds in John 6:36, 'You have seen me and still you do not believe.' You see, you can have your emotions powerfully affected and yet not believe.

*Shared in the Holy Spirit* is perhaps the most difficult phrase of all. It is not the same as indwelt by the Holy Spirit, as in Romans 8:9. It means taken up in some way in partnership with the Holy Spirit, perhaps even used by him. In the Sermon on the Mount Jesus said:

> Many will say to me on that day, 'Lord, Lord, did we not prophesy in your name, and in your name drive out demons and perform many miracles?' Then I will tell them plainly, 'I never knew you. Away from me, you evil doers' (Mt 7:22–23).

It is possible to be used by God and not be a Christian.

You can *taste the goodness of the word of God*, you can sense the powers of the spoken word of God and experience the miraculous interventions of God in your life. You can *feel the powers of the coming age* – just as if there were an exposed live cable by your feet. You could go near it and a spark could leap the gap from the cable to your fingers. You could momentarily feel the power that was pulsating continuously through that cable. But only the cable is permanently connected to the power station, to the source of supply. You would have had only a temporary influence, on the side, as it were.

It is perhaps like the hundreds of people who pass through our services and become affected, to one degree or another, in the ways the writer of Hebrews has described here. People can come into congregations and feel a temporary influence of the gospel that is so convincing that they are in no doubt that the gospel is true. Then they just turn aside and say: 'I don't want anything to do with it.' That is what is being described in these verses. There is no change of heart. They have had a mild dose of the real thing, but it has only inoculated them against full conversion. This is warning us that we can have very high privileges, but we have a high responsibility to act on those privileges. It is telling us very solemnly that we can come within the gateway of the city of refuge and still perish, because we have never entered fully in. John Murray has said:

These passages advise us of forces that are operative in the kingdom of God and of the influences those forces may exert upon those who finally demonstrate that they have never been radically and savingly affected by them.

## Never savingly changed

Examples like Simon Magus or Judas Iscariot all fall within the category of people who were greatly affected by the gospel, but were never savingly changed by it. The statement that sums this up is in 2 Peter 2:22, which speaks of a dog returning to its vomit, and of a sow that is washed going back to her wallowing in the mud. The dog never had its nature changed, neither did the sow: there was only an external change in their lives. Bruce Milne says:

> Anyone who returns wholeheartedly to sin, renounces former Christian ways, manifests no remorse in so doing and continues in this apostasy to the end of his life, was, *despite initial appearance* never truly born of God.

The perseverance of the saints is not in spite of what we are. It is because we continue in the faith that we persevere. The true explanation of those who fall away is in 1 John 2:19:

> They went out from us, but they did not really belong to us. For if they had belonged to us, they would have remained with us; but their going showed that none of them belonged to us.

There was no genuine faith from the start, despite all they professed.

If you and I do not persevere in the faith, what kind of God is it that we follow, whose will could be thwarted by ours? What kind of Saviour do we trust? Are not his mighty incarnation, his radiant and holy life, his infinitely valuable death on the cross, and his all-victorious resurrection enough to guarantee that we will get into heaven? The gospel we preach magnifies the irresistible and keeping grace of God, that will bring all his own to heaven.

If Jesus does indeed 'save to the uttermost all who come to God by him' then let this truth affect you radically and visibly.

*Stop idling!* The Christian life is no quiet life, no passive and indolent existence. It is intended to be a life of dynamic and energetic activity, a determination to pursue God and to live productively for his glory.

*Be liberated!* Shake off nervous introspection and the anxious 'pulse-taking' of a spiritual hypochondriac. Realize your security in God and allow that realization to set you free to serve him and minister to others.

*Be obedient!* All the truths we have surveyed have not been to provide excuses to live careless and indifferent lives, but rather to supply you with the greatest incentives to please God and obediently implement his will in your day-to-day pilgrimage to your certain goal. Go for gold!

*Be optimistic!* Never give up in despair over a backsliding friend, and never despair of yourself. Be humble, but confident. You will make it to the end, and praise God, so will your friend.

> Therefore, my dear brothers, stand firm. Let nothing move you. Always give yourselves fully to the work of the Lord, because you know that your labour in the Lord is not in vain' (1 Cor 15:58).

## Questions on perseverance

Q: Is it unnatural for a Christian ever to wonder if he is saved?

A: No. Most (all?) Christians have at some time doubted their salvation. But your very concern over it is almost certainly an indication that you *are* saved. Why else would you bother?

Q: Did Paul leave sanctification out of the 'golden chain of salvation' in Romans 8:29 because glorification does not depend on sanctification?

A: The thief on the cross had no opportunity to be sanctified, but he was saved. His glorification did not hinge on his inward holiness. Our perseverance does not ultimately depend on the level of our sanctification. We must persevere in faith, but holiness of life is very difficult to gauge and at some points may seem to be non-existent. Holiness is crucial – God has elected us 'to good works' (Eph 2:10). Holiness affects rewards, but salvation depends ultimately on grace and God, not us.

Q: If some can come so near as to have the experiences of Hebrews 6:4–6 and still not be saved at the end, how can any of us know we have been saved?

A: The only answer to that is by looking to Christ. Our assurance is not based in the last analysis on our experiences or obedience; it is based on Christ and what he has done. A Christian ought to have little difficulty in knowing that he is saved just by looking to Christ and what he's done. Such looking to Jesus has an accompanying witness of the Holy Spirit to the heart. No man can call Jesus 'Lord' except by the Holy Spirit. Do you look to Christ and say 'Jesus is my Lord'? When you look up to God, do you have a cry in your heart: 'Abba, Father'? Do you know he's your Father? Don't focus on yourself, focus on Jesus, focus on the Father. That's how I know I'm a Christian – primarily because I'm looking to Christ. That in fact is what the writer to the Hebrews majors on in the last half of chapter 6.

He does bolster them up by pointing out that they have suffered and endured so much: he was encouraged by that, but he will not let them base their assurance on what they have performed in their Christian life. He wants them to see what their hope is in the promises of God: 'Let us fix our eyes on Jesus, the author and perfector of our faith' (Heb 12:2). Assurance is derived primarily and sufficiently from Christ and only secondarily from any kind of change of life or obedience on our part.

Q: Does a backslider have to be restored while on earth in order to receive a place in glory?

A: Whatever a backslider is, he is not out of faith. This is proved by the fact that no one is more miserable on earth than a backslider. He can fully go back in all external appearances, but he is miserable because the seed of faith is within him. It is like a spring of water in the earth. You can block up the hole with all kinds of filth and dirt, and the spring can apparently stop flowing. But one day it's going to push through again. Christians have the responsibility to do what God has told them: 'As long as it's called today exhort one another daily, lest some of you become hardened through the deceitfulness of sin.' If we use the means that God has given – exhortation, rebuke, admonition, and even church discipline – and if he is genuinely a child of God, he will be restored.

Q: What is the unforgiveable sin? Can a Christian ever commit it?

A: The term Jesus used is the 'blasphemy against the Holy Spirit'. 'Blasphemy' meaning 'to speak evil against'. The Pharisees were attributing to the devil the works Jesus was performing in the power of the Spirit. The blasphemy against the Holy Spirit, therefore, is akin to the terms in Hebrews 10:29, namely, to trample under foot the Son of God, to treat as an unholy thing the blood of the covenant that sanctified him, and to insult the Spirit of grace. It is the mentality of an avowed, wilful, knowing rejection of the Holy Spirit's teaching, instruction, promptings, leading, conviction – a deliberate rejection of all of that. A Christian can never do that. The love of God is within us and there is a sin that we cannot commit. As John Murray said: 'There are certain types of unfaithfulness the Christian cannot commit.' And one type is trampling under foot the Son of God. However far a Christian may go, however much he may backslide, he cannot wilfully and knowingly trample under foot the preciousness of the blood of Christ, and say: 'No, Holy Spirit! I don't want anything to do with you or your religion again!'

Q: Is it possible for someone to have and use the gifts of the Holy Spirit and not be saved?

A: Not only can the Holy Spirit use graceless Christians in the gifts of the Spirit – he can also use non-Christians. Many will say to Jesus on the judgement day; 'Lord, Lord, did we not prophesy in your name, and in your name drive out demons and perform many miracles?' (Mt 7:22). Judas Iscariot, presumably, went out on all the missions with the apostles and was given along with them the ability to preach and to do miraculous works.

He came back with the rest of them saying: 'Lord, even the demons submit to us in your name' (Lk 10:17). Jesus said: 'Do not rejoice that the spirits submit to you, but rejoice that your names are written in heaven' (Lk 10:20).

Our security in the Christian life is not dependent on any gifts or abilities, even if given by the Holy Spirit. The least graces are better security for heaven than the most powerful gifts. The Holy Spirit may temporarily use non-Christians in works and gifts.

Q: Can you explain 2 Peter 1:5 – the exhortation to 'add to our faith'? How does this bear on perseverance?

A: The opening verses (1–4) of 2 Peter 1 speak about what God has done for us ('his divine power has given us everything we need for life and godliness'). The promises of God, all his resources, are at our disposal. Therefore verse 5 says: 'Get cracking! Make every effort to build – add to – furnish out – your faith' – as a couple would when they move into a house, first cleaning it out and then furnishing and decorating. Peter is saying: 'Here you are in the house of salvation. The house is swept clean. Well, now furnish it out!' The reason is (v. 10): 'Be all the more eager to make your calling and election sure for if you do these things, you will never fall, and you will receive a rich welcome into the eternal kingdom of our Lord and Saviour Jesus Christ.' Our salvation is not conditional on our obedience to verses 5 to 9, but our sense of welfare, well-being and that kind of 'rich welcome' are. Do you want Jesus to say to you on that day: 'Well done, good and faithful servant'? Well, for this reason, make every effort to furnish out your faith.

Q: Is it possible for a Christian to commit suicide? If so, how does that affect his standing before God?

A: It is very hard to understand the mind of a suicide, but perhaps more people than we may suspect have, in depression, entertained the thought. That does not mean that faith in Christ has died within them. It does not mean that the suicide has necessarily died outside the faith. Judas Iscariot, by contrast, seems to have died outside the faith; he had remorse for what he had done, but no repentance.

Peter, who denied Jesus and went away, was different, for he wept bitterly. There is no indication that Judas was repentant at the last. He died the apostate, unbelieving suicide's death, the death of a man in absolute despair. He is different from the Christian. Suicide is horrendous, but a Christian may not be in complete control of his faculties – for example, through the debilitating effects of prolonged mental trouble. Many factors drive a person towards suicide, but we are not warranted to say that such a person must have been an unbeliever. Their faith may have been too low to encourage them out of that depression, but not so low as to be non-existent.

Q: God does not base salvation on our works, but what place does he give to works in the Christian life?

A: A very high place indeed. Hebrews 6 is a rebuke to those who are lapsing from an energetic outworking of their faith. 'Let us leave the elementary teachings about Christ and go on to maturity' (6:1). His concept of maturity is a fruitful life of blessing to others – the life he delineates in Hebrews 13 by all his practical exhortations. '[We are] created in Christ Jesus to do good works, which God prepared in advance for us to do' (Eph 2:10). The practical thrust of all Paul's letters exhorts us to fruitfulness and energy in the Christian life. The *motive* for such exertion is not that our salvation hangs in the balance if we do not put our backs into it. It is precisely because our salvation is secure that we do and always want to 'give ourselves fully to the Lord'. (1 Cor 15:58). If I thought that there were some uncertainty about my salvation, I think I would give up. But if I know I am saved, that makes me all the keener for the Lord.

# For Further Reading

Among the many books relevant to the subjects covered in these pages are the following:

*General books on God and grace*
J. I. Packer *Knowing God* (Hodder & Stoughton).
J. I. Packer *Evangelism and the Sovereignty of God* (IVP).
A. W. Pink *The Sovereignty of God* (Banner of Truth).
D. A. Carson *Divine Sovereignty and Human Responsibility* (Marshall Morgan & Scott).
S. B. Ferguson *The Christian Life: a doctrinal introduction* (Hodder & Stoughton).
E. F. Kevan *Salvation* (Evangelical Press).

*Reference books*
B. J. Milne *Know the Truth* (IVP).
L. Berkhof *Systematic Theology* (Banner of Truth).
L. Berkhof *A Summary of Christian Doctrine* (Banner of Truth).

*Historical background*
For a celebrated collection of the statements of many of the major Reformed writers of the 16th and 17th centuries, see the volume *Reformed Dogmatics* by Heinrich Heppe (Baker Book House, USA).

*Specific themes*
(1) Man
For an excellent general survey of what the Bible says, and what Christians have thought down the centuries, see *The Christian View of Man* by H. D. McDonald (Marshall Morgan & Scott). On Marxism, see *The Challenge of Marxism* by Klaus Bockmuehl (IVP)

and *Karl Marx* by David Lyon (IVP/Lion). On existentialism and humanism, see the books listed in McDonald (above) and *Christianity: the true humanism* by J. I. Packer and T. Howard (Word). On the image of God in man, see McDonald and, for a more detailed study, *Man: the image of God* by G. C. Berkouwer (Studies in Dogmatics; IVP). See also *Sin* by G. C. Berkouwer (Studies in Dogmatics; Eerdmans). On holiness and wrath, see: (a) *The Cross in the New Testament* by L. Morris (Paternoster); (b) Volume 4 of *God, Revelation and Authority* by C. F. H. Henry (Word Books); and (c) *The Book of Leviticus* by G. Wenham (New International Commentary Series; Marshall Morgan & Scott). On Romans 1, see the multivolume series on Romans by D. M. Lloyd-Jones (Banner of Truth). For two classic works on man's condition, see *The Bondage of the Will* by Martin Luther and *The Freedom of the Will* by Jonathan Edwards.

(2) Election
G. C. Berkouwer *Election* (Studies in Dogmatics; Eerdmans).
B. B. Warfield *Biblical Foundations* (IVP; essay on 'Predestination').

(3) The cross
J. Murray *Redemption accomplished and applied* (Banner of Truth).
D. M. Lloyd-Jones *God's Way of Reconciliation* on Ephesians 2 (Banner of Truth).
J. Owen *The Death of Death in the Death of Christ* (Banner of Truth).
D. M. Lloyd-Jones *The Cross* (Kingsway Publications).
J. I. Packer *What did the cross achieve?* (Tyndale Bulletin, 1974).

(4) Grace
J. Cheeseman and others *The Grace of God in the Gospel* (Banner of Truth).
J. Boice *The Grace of God* (Baker Book House).

(5) Perseverance
D. M. Lloyd-Jones *Assurance* on Romans 5 (Banner of Truth).
D. M. Lloyd-Jones *The Final Perseverance of the Saints* on Romans 8:17-39 (Banner of Truth).

# God Meant it for Good

by R. T. Kendall

*Large format paperback*

*'When I came to Westminster Chapel at the age of forty-one I thought, "Surely I am ready now." But in a matter of months I could sense that I was still in the process of being prepared. That was most humbling indeed. There is a kind of preparation that cannot be found in university . . . it is that which God sovereignly ordains for a specific purpose and which drives us to our knees and to tears.'*

R. T. Kendall, Minister of Westminster Chapel in the heart of London, here reveals from the biblical story of Joseph how God works for those he loves.

Here we see the young and impetuous Joseph develop through sometimes painful and trying experience into a mature man willing to leave his own vindication with God. As we see Joseph learn what it means to forgive others totally—from the heart—we discover some of the wonderful ways in which our patient, loving God prepares us for his service.

k Kingsway Publications